IT'S OKAY TO BE THE BOSS

IT'S OKAY TO BE THE BOSS

THE STEP-BY-STEP GUIDE TO BECOMING THE MANAGER YOUR EMPLOYEES NEED

BRUCE TULGAN

Collins

An Imprint of HarperCollinsPublishers

The names and identifying characteristics of the individuals featured throughout this book have been changed to protect their privacy. In some cases, composite characters have been created.

HarperCollins books may be purchased for educational, business, or sales promotional use. For information, please write: Special Markets Department, HarperCollins Publishers, 10 East 53rd Street, New York, NY 10022.

FIRST EDITION

Designed by Laura Lindgren

Printed on acid-free paper

Library of Congress Cataloging-in-Publication Data is available upon request.

ISBN–13: 978–0–06–112136–4

07 08 09 10 11   ID/RRD   10 9 8 7 6 5 4 3 2 1

This book is dedicated to Debby Applegate

Contents

IT'S OKAY TO BE THE BOSS

CHAPTER 1

The Undermanagement Epidemic

You walk into your local video store. On your way in, you notice two employees standing outside the door talking. One of them is lighting another cigarette; they've been there for a while. Inside, you see that the one employee behind the counter is too busy to help you find the DVD you want. When you find where the DVD is supposed to be, you realize the wrong DVD has been shelved behind the case. In frustration, you settle on another choice and go to the counter to check out. Of course, it takes forever to check out. As you leave, you silently curse the terrible service and think to yourself, "This place is terrible. They've got to start hiring better employees in this store!"

It is tempting to look at this problem and blame the employees, or the entire enterprise. But the real cause is hiding behind the scenes: the manager. It is the manager's job to keep track of what's going on in that store and make sure that all the work is getting done on a consistent basis. How? By managing the people who work there! By telling the employees what to do and how to do it, by monitoring and measuring and documenting their performance, by solving problems quickly, and by singling people out for reward when they do a great job. That's what managing is.

Managing is a sacred responsibility. If you are the boss, it is your responsibility to make sure everything goes well. You have to make sure all the work is getting done very well, very fast all day long. If you are the boss, employees look to you first when they need something, or when they want something, or when something is going wrong. If there's a problem, you are the solution. If you are the boss, you are the one everyone is counting on.

But too many leaders, managers, and supervisors are failing to lead, manage, and supervise. They simply do not take charge on a day-to-day basis. They fail to spell out expectations every step of the way, track performance constantly, correct failure, and reward success. They are afraid to, or they don't want to, or they just don't know how to. All across the workplace, at all levels of organizations in every industry, there is a shocking and profound lack of daily guidance, direction, feedback, and support for employees. This is what I call "undermanagement"—the opposite of micromanagement.

Show me a case of bad customer service—like the video store I described—and I'll show you a case of undermanagement. In fact, show me just about any problem in any workplace and I'll show you a case of undermanagement. Follow the trail into the workplace, behind the scenes: What went wrong with the response to Hurricane Katrina or the failure to bolster the New Orleans levees beforehand? What went wrong with the loss of personal data of millions of veterans at the VA? Data theft from credit card companies? Jayson Blair and the "made-up news" scandal at the *New York Times*? Dan Rather and the "National Guard" debacle? Other corporate stars gone wild? What went wrong at Enron? Arthur Andersen? Tyco? Medical mishaps?

Pension deficits? Most airline delays? Whose job was it to make things go right? Whoever it is, that person has a boss. The boss is in charge. The boss is to blame. For what? For failing to *make sure* in the first place that the employees did their jobs properly.

Undermanagement is costing organizations a fortune every day. It robs so many employees of the chance to have positive experiences in the workplace, reach greater success, and earn more of what they need and want. It causes managers to struggle and suffer and deliver suboptimal results. It sours dealings with vendors and customers. And it costs society in so many ways. Undermanagement is not a household word like micromanagement, but it should be because its impact makes micromanagement look like a molehill.

The Undermanagement Epidemic: Hiding in Plain Sight

Back in 1993, I started investigating the work attitudes of Generation X (born 1965–1977), those of my own generation who were then just entering the workforce. Companies started inviting me to speak at their conferences, train their managers, observe their operations, interview their leaders, conduct focus groups with their employees. At first, I was focused exclusively on generational issues. I'd go into a company, interview their young employees, and then hold a seminar with the leaders and managers to share what the young employees had to say. It was usually the same basic story: "Your young workers feel like they don't get enough direction from their managers. They want more training. They want more support and guidance. They want more coaching. They want more feedback." I didn't realize it then, but the Generation Xers were really telling me that they were being undermanaged.

Like clockwork, one or more of the experienced workers would say something like "Son, welcome to the workplace. We all want someone to hold our hand and nobody is going to do that for you. When I started out, it was sink or swim every step of the way. If nobody told you what to do, you figured out what to do and you did it. Then you waited for your boss to notice you. No news was good news. If something went wrong, then you'd hear from your boss. Over time, you earn some seniority and the system takes care of you. It's no different now. These Generation Xers need to do what we all did. Pay your dues and climb the ladder." What these experienced workers were really telling me was that undermanagement had been the norm for as long as they could remember.

Although undermanagement was hiding in plain sight right before my eyes, it took me years to really start tuning in to the problem. Throughout the 1990s, as the tech boom turned into the dot-com boom, the GenX mind-set was spreading. And it was spreading not only to the next generation of young workers (Generation Y is like *Generation X on fast-forward with self-esteem on steroids*). By the time the dot-com boom went bust, it became increasingly obvious that what had first appeared to be a "Generation X thing" had become the mainstream employee attitude. The fact that Generation Xers had been in the vanguard of this shift was simply an accident of history. Something much larger was happening. The traditional long-term hierarchical employer-employee bond was morphing into a short-term transactional relationship. By the first years of the twenty-first century, workers of all ages were making it clear that without credible long-term promises from employers, they were no longer content to labor quietly and obediently in a sink-or-swim environment. The less faith they had in "the system" to take care of them in the long term, the more they expected from their immediate supervisors in the short term. As the workplace was becoming more and more high pressure, the workforce was becoming more and more high maintenance.

Since the mid-1990s, I've had a front-row seat from which to study workplace dynamics. I've spent most of my time training managers at all levels: tens of thousands of managers, from CEOs to frontline supervisors, in just about every industry—retail, health care, research, finance, aerospace, software, manufacturing, the public sector, even nonprofits, you name it. Managers' successes thrill me. Their failures break my heart. Their challenges are my challenges.

I've spent so much time behind the scenes in so many organizations that I can tell you this: most problems could be avoided altogether or solved quickly by a highly engaged hands-on manager, by a boss who accepts her authority and the responsibility that goes along with it. This is the boss who says, "Great news, I'm the boss! And I'm going to try really hard to be a great one!" Unfortunately, highly engaged managers are rare. Frankly, most bosses are not so great. Many struggle to be better. Some don't even bother to struggle. Most bosses are so hands-off they mostly don't manage unless they absolutely must.

Why is that?

It's Getting Harder to Manage People

It's always been hard to manage people. Managers have always been stuck in the middle between the employer and the employee, trying to negotiate their competing needs and expectations. Most managers, like most human beings, have probably always gone out of their way to avoid those conflicts. One of the legacies of the old-fashioned workplace (that of the postwar myth about dues paying and ladder climbing for job security) is hands-off leadership based on sink-or-swim followership. In the old long-term hierarchical model (the pyramid organization chart), followers took for granted their managers' authority and the authority of the employer. As a result, followers were more likely to figure out what to do and do it, making lots of mistakes along the way, no doubt. But there was more room back then for waste and inefficiency. Not anymore.

Nowadays, it's a whole lot harder to manage people. Today, the world is highly interconnected, fiercely competitive, knowledge driven, and global. Markets are chaotic, resource needs are unpredictable, and employers are geared for constant change. As a result, employers must be lean and flexible in order to survive, and individuals must be increasingly aggressive in order to take care of themselves and their families. Employees are less likely to trust the "system" or the organization to take care of them over time and thus less likely to make immediate sacrifices in exchange for promises of long-term rewards. They are more likely to disagree openly with employers' missions, policies, and decisions and challenge employment conditions and established reward systems. As a result of all of these changes, most employees are much less obedient to employers' rules and supervisors' instructions.

Traditional sources of authority are also being steadily supplanted by new sources. Seniority, age, rank, and established practice are diminishing. Organization charts are flatter; layers of management have been removed. Reporting relationships are more temporary; more employees are being managed by short-term project leaders, instead of "organization-chart" managers. On the rise as sources of authority are more transactional forms such as control of resources, control of rewards, and control of work conditions. Employees look to their immediate supervisors to meet their basic needs and expectations and freely make demands of their managers. Managers who cannot meet these needs have less and less authority in the eyes of employees.

Meanwhile, most managers, like everybody else, have more tasks and responsibilities of their own, along with more administrative duties. Even so, managerial spans of control—the number of employees officially reporting to each supervisor—have increased. More managers are managing employees working in locations remote from the manager. Plus the breadth and complexity of the work being done by the employees reporting to each manager have also expanded in most cases.

Taken together, the changes in the workplace have brought about a fundamental shift in norms and values that go to the core of the employer-employee relationship. Here's the problem: Most managers still avoid conflict. Most still lack any special aptitude for leadership and receive little training in the basic tactics of effective supervision. And the legacy of leadership in most organizations great and small is still hands-off: "Here's the mission. Figure it out. Wait for us to notice you. We'll let you know if you do something wrong and the system will reward you the same as everyone else."

Management Has Been Going in the Wrong Direction

For too long now, the pendulum of management thinking, books, and training has swung so far in exactly the wrong direction, toward hands-off management.

Ever since *The One Minute Manager*, by Kenneth Blanchard and Spencer Johnson, too many management thinkers have been trying to sell easy solutions to the great challenge of leading and empowering people. Of course, that ingenious book got it half right: After all, what is "goal setting" if not spelling out expectations? What is "praising" if not singling people out for special reward? What is "scolding" if not pointing out failures and taking corrective action? But Blanchard and Johnson also got if half wrong: managing takes a whole lot more than one minute.

Likewise, look at Marcus Buckingham's best-selling books such as *First, Break All the Rules*. What makes this book so great, like *The One Minute Manager*, is its intensive focus on the immediate supervisory relationship—that is, on the role of the boss. The problem with Buckingham, like most in this genre, is the naive insistence that employees do their best work when they are free to manage themselves. The best way to get employees "engaged" at work, these false nice guys argue, is to put employees on assignments they enjoy and give them lots of praise. The only problem is, who is going to do all the work no one enjoys?

The recent widespread use of the term "engagement" is just another way of invoking the vastly misunderstood concept of "empowerment." Empowerment has been widely misunderstood ever since Douglas McGregor gave us Theory X and

Theory Y: Theory X says that workers are best motivated by external sources such as fear, coercion, and tangible rewards. Theory Y says that workers are best motivated by sources internal to themselves such as desire, belief, and the quest for self-actualization. Nearly all the relevant research indicates that people are actually motivated by both internal *and* external factors. Nonetheless, Theory Y has been the main ingredient in the "empowerment" literature for several decades, to the nearly total exclusion of Theory X. The result is that "false empowerment" has become the prevailing approach in management thinking, books, and training. In the "false empowerment" approach, managers should not keep close track of employees and they definitely should not zero in on employee failures. Employees should be made to feel they "own" their work and should be set free to make their own decisions. Managers are merely facilitators, there to align the natural talents and desires of employees with fitting roles in the workplace. Managers should not tell people how to do their jobs, but rather let employees come up with their own methods. The idea is, make employees feel good inside and results will take care of themselves.

This false empowerment approach dovetails with broader social/cultural/workplace trends away from hierarchy. We "question authority" at work, in the family, and everywhere else. The wishful thinking that "nobody needs to be in charge" is underwritten by this larger discourse.

But face it. Somebody *is* in charge and employees will "be held accountable." Employees do not have the "power" to do things their own way in the workplace. They are not free to ignore tasks they don't like. They are not free to do as they please. Rather, employees are free only to make their own decisions within defined guidelines and parameters that are determined by others according to the strict logic of the enterprise at hand. Responsibility without sufficient direction and support is not empowerment. It is downright negligent.

The fact that false empowerment just doesn't work is evidenced by the fact that nearly every organization I know of has tried one strategy after another either to force managers to lead with a stronger hand or to somehow end-run the management part of leadership.

Business leaders often say to me privately that they hope to solve the management problem with technology: "Computers don't argue, complain, or make demands!" Others tell me they are hoping to solve the problem with outsourcing and immigration: "Workers from more traditional cultures still have the old-fashioned work ethic." There are obvious limits to the technology, immigration, and outsourcing solutions, but these strategies are popular precisely because they are efforts to sidestep the seemingly intractable challenge of actually getting managers to manage employees today.

And, of course, they are just the tip of the iceberg. What are the three leading trends in human-capital management today? The new version of management by objective, forced ranking, and pay for performance.

New version of "management by objective." Managers at all levels today are given performance objectives (referred to as "numbers" because they are usually articulated in numbers) for every dimension of their operations. The very worthy intention is to place the focus on concrete, measurable outcomes. The problem is that usually the numbers serve as a trigger for cascading recrimination (or praise), even though what gets measured is often not tied directly to actions in the control of individual employees. Without step-by-step directions communicated clearly at every level of the chain of command, these objectives are often little more than wishes.

Forced ranking. Because most managers are so reluctant to make distinctions between and among employees and single out individuals for blame or reward, most leading organizations are moving to some form of "forced ranking." This is the practice whereby managers are required to make candid evaluations of every employee according to a tight distribution of grades such as A, B, and C. This practice was made famous by Jack Welch, the CEO of GE for some twenty years. Sadly, while evaluation and differentiation are key, this is an exercise in annual guesswork unless managers are monitoring, measuring, and documenting every employee's performance on an ongoing basis. Once a year doesn't do the trick.

Pay for performance. This is by far the biggest trend in compensation: decreasing the amount of employee pay that is fixed and increasing the amount that is contingent on performance. I applaud the notion of differential rewards based on differential performance. I think you get what you pay for and you should deliver for what you get paid. The problem is that pay for performance works only when managers spell out for each employee exactly what the employee needs to do (concrete actions within the control of the employee) to get paid more and exactly what the employee could do to get paid less. Then the manager needs to monitor and measure and document each employee's actual performance (concrete actions) on an ongoing basis. When managers don't do this critical work, differential rewards are given out, but the connection between reward and individual performance is not clearly made. So the system is perceived as capricious and unfair. Over and over again, I have seen pay-for-performance initiatives result in disastrous morale because managers failed to do the necessary work.

These are three of the fastest-growing trends in management, central to the new high-pressure workplace in which high performance is the only option. But there is a "cart before the horse" problem here. The irony is that each of these strategies is intended to make up for the fact that managers don't take a stronger hand. Yet each of these strategies depends for its success on managers taking a stronger hand, and they fail miserably when managers are weak. That's why these strategies have such mixed reputations.

Yet another popular tactic to try to end-run management is to hire your way out of managing. There are numerous hiring systems that offer elaborate testing and interviewing protocols with the goal of screening out all job applicants who are not likely to be self-starting high performers. I am a firm believer in using good hiring systems (Lou Adler's is the best in-house system; on the web, Monster is second to none). The problem is that you cannot hire an unlimited number of superstars. Besides, even superstars need to be managed.

Here's the punch line: there is no end run around the management part of leadership. Those in leadership positions simply must take charge of their people: give orders, track performance, correct failure, and reward success, every step of the way. These are just the basics of managing people, and anything less is undermanagement.

Why Managers Don't Manage

Unfortunately, most managers have bought the false-empowerment philosophy that is constantly peddled in and out of the workplace. Most don't take a stronger hand when it comes to managing—they don't even perform the basic tasks of managing. Most managers undermanage. Why?

Let's go back to the manager of that video store at the beginning of this book. If you interviewed a manager like this one privately, as I do all the time in my research, he would say something like this: "Look, I have my own work to do. I don't have time to hold every employee's hand. And I shouldn't have to. I did the job for two years and nobody had to tell me what to do. I just did it. That's how I got to be the manager. I try to be hands-off unless something goes wrong. If I started bossing people around all of a sudden, they would think I turned into a big jerk. They would say, 'Don't tell me how to do my job; it's not fair; it's not my fault.' Mary would get mad and argue and make excuses. Joe would start crying. Sam would probably just fold his arms and listen stone-faced until I stop talking, and then he'd just walk away. Chris would agree with everything I said—'yes' me until I shut up. Maybe I'd end up firing Mary. Joe would probably quit. Maybe I'm just not a natural leader. I love retail, but I guess I am not so great at managing. I would probably cause more problems than I would solve. In the end, my boss would probably be mad that I didn't leave well enough alone."

This manager is in a real quandary. It is a quandary shared by leaders and managers everywhere I go. I ask managers every single day why they don't take a stronger hand when it comes to managing. They almost always give me the same reasons—I call them the top seven management myths in today's workplace.

#1. The Myth of Empowerment: The way to empower people is to leave them alone and let them manage themselves.

This is false empowerment, the number one myth in the workplace.

What is the reality? Almost everybody performs better with more guidance, direction, and support from a more experienced person.

So why do managers often second-guess their own instincts to take a stronger hand? Precisely because they have been ingrained with the mantras of false empowerment. When managers do take charge, employees often recite these same mantras, complaining, "Don't micromanage me!"

The funny thing is that most cases mistaken for micromanagement turn out to be undermanagement in disguise. Let me show you.

Case number one. The employee must check with his manager every step of the way in order to make very basic decisions or take very simple actions. Is this really a case of micromanagement? No. If an employee is unable to make very basic decisions or take very simple actions on his own, that's almost always because the manager has not prepared the employee in advance to do so. Someone has to tell him, "If A happens, do B. If C happens, do D. If E happens, do F." That's how you equip an employee to make decisions and take action. Someone has to tell the employee exactly what to do and how to do it. Someone has to make sure he understands how to accomplish his tasks and carry out his responsibilities. Someone has to equip the employee with the tools and techniques of the job. That someone is the manager.

Case number two. The employee makes decisions and takes actions without ever checking in with her manager. When the manager finds out about those decisions and actions, the employee gets in big trouble. Burned for taking initiative? Yes. Micromanagement? No. If an employee does not know where her discretion begins and ends, that's because the manager has not spelled out guidelines and parameters for the employee up front. Someone has to painstakingly clarify for her what is within her authority and what is not. Someone has to repeatedly spell out what she cannot and may not do. That someone is the manager.

Case number three. The manager remains tangled up with the employee's tasks or the employee gets tangled up with the manager's tasks—in the end, you just can't tell which tasks belong to the manager and which ones belong to the employee. Isn't that micromanagement? No. This is failure to delegate. Some work is hard to delegate, but if the work cannot be delegated properly, it is the manager's job to figure that out and act accordingly. Someone has to spell out exactly which tasks belong to the employee and which ones belong to the manager. Someone has to tell the employee up front in advance exactly what is to be done, where, when, and how. That someone is the manager.

All of these cases often misconstrued as "micromanagement" turn out to be cases of undermanagement. That's why I often say that micromanagement is a giant red herring. Is there even such a thing as "micromanagement" at all? Of course, some managers overdo it sometimes, but the vast majority underdo it. Real micromanagement, if it exists at all, is quite rare. Look at the basics of management: Delegate properly so each employee knows which tasks belong to him and him alone. Spell out exactly what is within his authority and what is not. Equip him with the tools and techniques of the job. That's not micromanagement, that's just plain management. Anything less is undermanagement.

What does real empowerment look like? If you want to truly empower people, then you simply must define the terrain on which they have power. That terrain consists of effectively delegated goals, with clear guidelines and concrete deadlines. Consistently articulating with every direct report the appropriate standards and expectations—what to do and how to do it—is the hard work of leading, managing, and supervising. Within clearly articulated parameters, a direct report has power. Limited power? Yes. But it also has the great virtue of being real power.

#2. The Myth of Fairness: The way to be fair is to treat everybody the same.

Where does this myth come from? First, the Human Resources/ EEO/Legal Department aversion to any kind of litigation risk has led to a blanket default presumption in the working world that differential treatment of employees is "against the rules." Second is the closely related political correctness that causes so many people to self-censor any mention of differences between and among individuals—even observable merit-based differences. Third is the popular misunderstanding of humanistic psychology and human development theory, which holds in essence that "we are all winners." The underlying theory is that because every person has innate value, we should treat everybody the same. That's only fair if you are running a commune.

The reality is that we are not all winners, as any one of your employees could tell you. Treating everybody the same, regardless of their behavior, is totally unfair.

Since the early 1990s, the self-improvement movement has made an odd shift away from "improving" one's self, toward feeling good about one's self, improved or not. The irony is that real human development comes precisely from helping people assess their performance honestly and helping them to improve, so they can earn the rewards they need and want. All the feel-good pretend-sameness becomes yet another excuse for managers to avoid monitoring and measuring performance, much less telling employees when they've failed and helping them improve. When managers do point out failures to employees, they are often met with resistance or strong emotions: "It's not my fault. Stop picking on me." That's when a lot of managers second-guess themselves and withdraw again.

Even worse, hiding behind false fairness means that most managers are unable or unwilling to provide employees with extra rewards when they do go the extra mile. I know a lot of managers who actually say to employees, "I really appreciate your extra effort, but I can't do something special for you. If I did that for you, I'd have to do that for everybody." Of course, you can't do everything for everybody, so most managers take the easy way out, which is rewarding nobody specially. The result: Low and mediocre performers enjoy roughly the same rewards as the high performers. Limited resources for rewards are further watered down by trying to spread them around equally. High performers grow frustrated and angry. The upshot: Managers fail to give the best employees the flexibility they need to continue working so hard and so smart, and they deprive themselves of a key tool for motivating employees.

What's truly fair? Do more for some people and less for others, based on what they deserve—based on their performance.

#3. The Myth of the Nice Guy: The only way to be strong is to act like a jerk, but I want to be a "nice guy."

Lots of managers act like jerks. That doesn't mean they are strong. It just means they are acting like jerks.

What is the reality? Real "nice guy" managers do what it takes to help employees succeed so those employees can deliver great service for customers and earn more rewards for themselves.

Sometimes when managers hear me say, "It's okay to be the boss," they picture bosses they've known in the past whom they remember as being particularly, well, "bossy"—arbitrary, out of line, loud, mean, and even abusive. Let me be very clear: When I say, "It's okay to be the boss," that is *not* what I'm talking about.

Why do bosses sometimes act like jerks? Some people revel in being at the top of the heap—it is an ego trip for them. It makes them feel important. It gives them a chance to lord it over other people. For them, it's the workplace version of schoolyard bullying. It is also irresponsible and damaging.

Some bosses are jerks out of pure negligence: they don't really know what's going on, but make important decisions anyway. These are the jerks who do not give employees feedback on their performance until they fail terribly, and then impose very serious consequences. These are the jerks who use their authority as the boss, but in all the wrong ways at all the wrong times, without ever doing the hard work of managing people.

Then there is the surprisingly widespread phenomenon of "false nice guy complex." The "false nice guy" managers refuse to make decisions, give orders, and hold people accountable. They tell themselves that they are doing so because they don't want to be a "jerk," or they want to be "nice." They convince themselves that it is somehow *not* okay to be the boss. The wielding of authority by one person over another seems wrong to them. This is another misunderstanding that flows out of an egalitarian impulse: All people are equal in the cosmos, and therefore one person should not claim superiority or call for the obedience of another in any relationship. That's beautiful.

Really? Then why do you go into a restaurant and start giving orders to the waiter? Because you are paying the restaurant for service and food. The waiter, on the other hand, is being paid. No hard feelings. It's a transactional relationship. In the same way, your authority as the boss at work does not require some claim of superiority in the cosmos. Employment is a transactional relationship, just like a customer relationship. Those whom you manage are being paid to do the job. That is the ultimate source of your authority, plain and simple. No hard feelings.

The irony is that false nice guys tend to soft-pedal their authority so much that things are bound to go wrong. Then they get frustrated and angry and tend to act like jerks: arbitrary, out of line, loud, mean, and even abusive. The difference is that false nice guys tend to feel terribly guilty after behaving this way. So what do they do? They go back to soft-pedaling their authority, without ever realizing that they are caught in a vicious cycle.

Are they really being "nice guy" managers by failing to provide the direction, support, and coaching that employees need in order to succeed?

In truth, they are simply letting themselves off the hook, to avoid the uncomfortable tension that comes with being stuck between the boardroom and the front lines—the one who has to negotiate the competing needs and desires of the employer and the employee. They are refusing to take responsibility for their authority, which has real consequences that are anything but nice: Problems occur, sometimes big ones. When problems are not dealt with, sometimes they turn into disasters. Sometimes career-damaging or career-ending disasters. Not so nice. The best way to avoid being a jerk is to accept your legitimate authority and be comfortable using that authority legitimately.

#4. The Myth of the Difficult Conversation: Being hands-off is the way to avoid confrontations with employees.

Most managers find that the most painful and damaging aspect of managing is when they must have very difficult conversations, even confrontations, with employees about some problem or another. They believe that being a strong manager requires or even causes these confrontations, whereas being a weak manager allows them to avoid these confrontations.

What is the reality? Being a weak manager makes these confrontations inevitable, whereas being a strong manager means these confrontations rarely occur, and when they do happen they are not so painful after all.

One of my main goals when I'm training managers is to help them get over their fear of confronting employees. Our research shows that the primary reason why so many management conversations are so very difficult is precisely because they are so rare. When management conversations happen only on special occasions, they tend to be very difficult. Why?

- Neither the manager nor the employee is experienced at having management conversations, so neither is very good at it.

- The manager has not been making expectations clear, so much of the conversation comes as a big unpleasant surprise to the employee.

- These conversations usually happen when a problem absolutely must be dealt with, so the conversations are more likely to become heated. Plus, solving a problem after the fact is a whole lot more difficult than preventing it in advance.

- Because the manager is out of the loop, he usually doesn't have all the facts and thus has less confidence in his point of view and fewer resources with which to make his points and respond to employee push-backs.

This approach is a lot like losing your temper. You finally decide to "put your foot down" about one or more issues and problems that you've let slide. You call a team meeting and pronounce: "People have to start coming in on time and taking shorter breaks, and this time I'm serious. And by the way, all the chitchat in the office has to stop. I want people focused on

their work!" Maybe then you might ask that one problem employee who has been driving you crazy to follow you into your
office and tell him that he'd better shape up, or, better yet, that
he's fired. That day you might go home thinking, "I just did
some managing!" Then the next day you come back to work and
go right back to your hands-off status quo.

If your version of taking charge is turning from "nice guy"
into "tough guy" on a dime, then there is a good chance you
will seem like a jerk. Not only that, but people are not likely
to take you seriously. They might think that you can't or won't
enforce your new pronouncements ... or will ultimately cool off
and forget about the whole thing. Maybe you won't be any good
at these confrontations and they won't go well; maybe people
will push back and you'll crumble. Maybe people will be angry,
or they'll snicker and scoff, or they won't like you anymore.
The whole thing will be awkward and uncomfortable and painful—and then, after all that, maybe your efforts to take charge
won't work anyway.

Taking charge in any meaningful and lasting way is a lot
like getting in shape physically. It is a long tedious process. It
requires fundamental changes in your behavior, changes that
become new habits. There are no shortcuts. It takes time to see
results. You'll still have some difficult conversations and even
some extraordinary confrontations, but many fewer, and only
when necessary. It takes guts to take charge and be a strong
manager, but probably not for the reasons you think. Don't
be afraid of a few difficult confrontations. Be afraid of a long,
slow, tedious transition that will radically change your habits,
your role, and your relationships at work from now on and for-
evermore. If you can't muster that courage, then maybe you
shouldn't be the boss.

#5. The Myth of Red Tape: Managers are prevented from being strong because there are many factors beyond their control—red tape, corporate culture, senior management, limited resources.

Managers tell me every day that despite their best efforts, they are held back by rules and red tape and contracts. By the way, some managers hide behind this challenge as an excuse to not manage. And almost always, right beside them, in the very same organization with the very same rules and red tape and contracts, there are lots of managers who find ways to work within and around the rules and red tape and contracts. It's difficult, but they do it anyway because that is their job.

How do you work within and around the rules, red tape, and contracts? I am a lawyer technically. So let me tell you what lawyers do when confronted with rules and red tape and contracts. They learn the rules and red tape and contracts backward and forward. And then they work them. What else is there to do? Learn the rules and work them.

Are you worried about being sued? There are many impermissible reasons for distinguishing between and among employees. Performance is not one of them. As long as you can demonstrate that any rewards or detriments to employees are based solely on their work performance, there is no basis for a claim of unlawful discrimination. Find an ally who can help you learn the rules and work the rules: Someone in HR. Someone in legal. Someone in EEO. Someone in the union. Your boss.

Remember this: Of course, there will be things you *can't* do. Don't do them. If you do, you'll get in trouble. But often you can do things you didn't realize you could do, once you learn *how* do them. There are so many things you *can* do. You cannot remove every obstacle. But there are so many partial solutions that make such a big difference.

The myth is believing that the factors beyond your control are what make you feel powerless.

What is the reality? Focusing on what you can't control makes the most powerful person weak, whereas focusing intensely on what you can control—to the exclusion of what you cannot control—will always make you stronger.

The fact is, there are so many things in your control: you, your guts, your skill, your habits, and your time. You don't need anyone's permission to be strong. You don't need anyone's permission to talk to your employees more often—one-on-one—about the work each is doing. You don't need permission to set people up for success, to spell out expectations clearly every step of the way, to clarify goals and guidelines and deadlines. You don't need permission to monitor and measure and document performance every step of the way. You don't need permission to zero in on small problems immediately and solve them before they grow into larger problems. You don't need permission to try your best to steer more rewards to people who go the extra mile.

#6. The Myth of the Natural Leader: I am not "good at" managing.

The underlying theory here is that some people are natural leaders and therefore the best managers, whereas others are not natural leaders and are destined to be not-so-great managers.

What is the reality? Lots of natural leaders are not such great managers. The best managers are people—natural or not—who learn proven techniques, practice those techniques diligently until they become skills, and continue practicing them until they become habits.

Is there such a thing as natural leadership ability? Of course. Some people are visionary, charismatic, articulate, filled with ideas, and unusually energetic. They are motivators. They inspire. People want to follow them. But that doesn't necessarily make them good managers. More often, these great leaders succeed precisely when they are smart enough to hire great managers and let them do the crucial management part of leadership. Indeed, one of the most common stories I hear from managers in this scenario is how the natural leader often whirls into the workplace, distracting employees, exhilarating them, patting people on the back, making random decisions, building personal loyalty among the employees, spreading ideas and thoughts that create hopes and fears ... and then disappears, leaving the manager to clean up the mess.

I use the term "management" precisely to focus on the more mundane, but absolutely crucial, aspects of leadership: providing direction and guidance, holding people accountable, dealing with failure, and rewarding success. These are the basic elements of management that are way too often missing from leadership today. And these are the elements that are by far the most important when it comes to getting more work and better work out of employees and helping them earn more of what they need. I've learned from training tens of thousands of individuals that almost anyone can become a much better manager. How? Learn proven techniques. Then practice, practice, practice those techniques until they become skills (and then habits).

#7. The Myth of Time: There's isn't enough time to manage people.

This myth comes from the fact that there are only 168 hours in a week and you have zillions of demands on your time—you have your own tasks and responsibilities and projects besides your management obligations.

What is the reality? Since your time is so limited, you definitely don't have time to *not* manage people. Managers who try desperately to avoid spending time managing people always spend lots of time managing people anyway. That's because when a manager avoids spending time up front in advance making sure things go right, things always go wrong. Small problems pile up. Often, small problems fester unattended until they become so big that they cannot be ignored. By that point, the manager has no choice but to chase down the problems and solve them. In crisis, the manager is virtually guaranteed to be less efficient, a further waste of time. So these managers run around solving problems that never had to happen, getting big problems under control that should have been solved easily, recouping squandered resources, dealing with long-standing performance problems, feeling even more pressed for time. That means in all likelihood they will go right back to avoiding managing people, and the next time they'll make time for management is the next time there is another big problem to chase down and solve.

Remember that the time you spend managing is "high-leverage time." By managing, you engage the productive capacity of the people you manage. For every, say, fifteen-minute management conversation you have with an employee, you should be engaging hours or maybe days of that employee's productive capacity. If that fifteen-minute conversation is effective, that fifteen minutes of management should substantially improve the quality and output of the employee's work for hours or days. That's a good return on investment—that's why I call it "high-leverage time."

If you put your management time where it belongs and attend to the basics every step of the way, the time you do spend managing will be so much more effective. You'll start to see results right away. Very quickly, things will improve, and you'll start to get a lot of that time back on the other end.

The Hard Realities of Managing People

I know that for most people, being really hands-on requires a fundamental rethinking of the manager's role and the management relationship. Indeed, many participants in my seminars tell me, "Nobody has ever said this to me. I feel like you are giving me permission to manage, permission to be the boss. What a breath of fresh air." Of course, lots of participants tell me, "This is common sense. It is so basic. Managers have to manage, plain and simple. What were we thinking?" Indeed, much of what I am saying is basic common sense. Managers need to manage.

The funny thing is that about half of the participants in my seminars say just the opposite (at the beginning, anyway): "You must be crazy. This contradicts most everything I've ever read in management books and been taught in other management training classes." And they are right. Very few people out there are saying what I am saying.

Managing people in the real world is very, very difficult,

and there are no easy solutions. I know that most managers
are under a tremendous amount of pressure. Most managers
move into positions of supervisory responsibility because they
are very good at something, but *not* usually for the reason that
they are especially good at managing people. Once promoted,
most new managers receive very little in the way of effective
management training. And the management books and training that they *do* receive are dominated by the false empowerment approach. They rarely address the "hard" realities of
managing:

- You cannot always hire superstars. You have to hire the
  best person available, and often that person is in the middle
  of the talent spectrum, not at the top.

- When you do hire superstars, they can be even harder to
  manage than the mediocre people.

- Even if you set expectations clearly, sometimes employees
  don't achieve those expectations.

- Not everybody is a winner. Dealing with failure is a big
  part of managing.

- Employees can't always work in their areas of strength
  because there is lots of work to be done, and employees are
  hired to do what needs to be done.

- Employees don't always earn praise. And those who do
  earn praise usually want tangible rewards, not just praise.

In our training seminars, when I start talking about these
hard realities, managers start nodding their heads and listening

carefully. When I tell them that I don't have any easy answers because easy answers work only in fantasyland, more people start nodding. Then I promise them that I do have lots of very hard solutions that will take lots of guts, skill, time, and discipline to implement. That's when they know that I really have something to offer them. All I do in my seminars is teach frustrated managers to copy what the most effective managers are actually doing every day. I've trained tens of thousands of managers in the real world in the mundane techniques of strong, highly engaged, hands-on management. I hear back from managers that I've trained just about every day. And the word from the front line is: They are getting more out of employees and doing more for employees, one person at a time, one day at a time.

It's Okay to Be the Boss; Be a Great One

It's okay to be the boss. In fact, it's critical. The boss—at every level—is the most important person in the workplace today. Everybody is under more pressure. Employees are expected to work longer, harder, smarter, faster, and better. And employees are not about to wait around for long-term rewards. They rely on their immediate boss more than any other individual for meeting their basic needs and expectations at work, and for dealing with just about any issue that arises at work. They want to know, "What's the deal around here? What do you want from me? And what do I get for my hard work today?" The boss is the point of contact—but much more than that, on a daily basis, the boss defines the work experience. On this there is widespread consensus: In study after study, the number one factor in productivity, morale, and retention is the relationship between employees and their immediate boss.

So what are employees looking for in a boss?

Low performers are looking for a boss who is hands-off and tries to treat every employee the same. They want a boss who doesn't know who is doing what, where, why, when, and how, a boss who doesn't keep track, a boss who ignores performance problems. Low performers want a boss who doesn't tell them what to do and how to do it, who doesn't spell out expectations every step of the way. They want to be left alone to hide out and collect the same paycheck as everyone else, regardless of their low performance. Low performers are the great beneficiaries of undermanagement. They are drawn to undermanagers the way vermin are drawn to dark cold places.

On the other hand, high performers want a boss who is strong and highly engaged, who knows exactly who they are and exactly what they are doing every step of the way. High performers want a boss who lets them know that they are important and that their work is important. They want a boss who spells out expectations clearly, who teaches them the best practices, who warns them of pitfalls, who helps them solve small problems before they fester and grow, and who rewards them when they go the extra mile. High performers want a boss who will clear the low performers out of the way. They are always looking for strong managers who will set them up for success and, thereby, help them earn what they need and want from the job, every step of the way. Strong hands-on managers are like magnets for high performers.

What about the vast majority of employees who are somewhere in the middle between high performance and low? You will get out of them exactly what you put in—in almost exact proportion to how much technique, time, and energy you put into managing them.

If you are hands-off and treat everybody the same, you are treating your employees like low performers. You will undermanage most of them into a slow downward spiral. And you will attract more low performers who want to "work for you." If you are strong and highly engaged, you are treating your employees like high performers. You will manage most of them into a steady upward spiral. And high performers will beat down your door for the chance to work for you.

It comes down to this: What kind of employees do you want looking for you? What kind of boss are you going to be?

Be the boss who says, "Great news, I'm the boss! I consider that a sacred responsibility. I'm going to make sure that everything goes well around here. I'm going to help you get a bunch of work done very well, very fast, all day long. I'm going to set you up for success every step of the way. I'm going to spell out expectations for you every step of the way. I'm going to help you plan. I'm going to work with you to clarify goals, guidelines, and specifications. I'm going to help you break big deadlines into smaller time frames with concrete performance benchmarks. I'm going to go over standard operating procedures. I'm going to offer reminders. I'm going to provide checklists and other tools. I'm going to help you keep track of what you are doing and how you are doing it every step of the way. I'm going to help you monitor and measure and document your success every step of the way. I'm going to help you solve problems as soon as they occur, so they don't fester and grow into bigger problems. I'm going to help you find the shortcuts, avoid the pitfalls, and follow the best practices. Count on me. When you need something, I'm going to help you find it. When you want something, I'm going to help you earn it."

The rest of this book is meant to help you get past the myths and tackle the very real challenges that make it so hard to be a manager today. Yes, it's hard. Step up to the challenge.

It's okay to be the boss. Be a great one!

CHAPTER 2

Get in the Habit of Managing Every Day

You are working on a big project for your boss. You have been barricaded in your office for days trying to finish it. But that's nothing new. Your employees know you are always super busy. You've been managing this team—sixteen people now—for several years. They know how to do their jobs, so you pretty much leave them alone unless something comes up. Unfortunately, something always does. Today, a crisis forces you to come whirling out of your office, determined to solve it quickly so you can get back to your "real work." But solving the problem consumes most of your day. By the time you finally get back to your office, you are way behind schedule.

If this sounds like you, you are not alone. Most managers are so busy with their own "real work" that they think of their management work mostly as an extra burden. They avoid daily managing the way a lot of people avoid daily exercise. They manage only when they absolutely have to. As a result, they and their employees get out of shape, and unexpected problems crop up on a regular basis. When problems get out of control, these managers can no longer avoid their responsibility and they spring into action. By that point, however, they have a very difficult task on their hands: they are trying to run ten miles when they are completely out of shape.

I call this phenomenon—managing only when it can no longer be avoided— "management by special occasion." Most of these "special occasions" are big problems that need solving, but there are other special occasions too: assigning a new project to an employee, communicating a change from on high to the team, or recognizing a huge success. In the absence of some "special occasion," though, most managers simply don't manage.

The only alternative to management by special occasion is getting in the habit of managing every day.

The First Person You Need to Manage Every Day Is Yourself

If you were in poor physical shape, would you go for a ten-mile run? No. First, you might start training by taking a walk every day. After a few weeks, you might walk a little faster and longer and begin gaining some muscle tone. Over time, you start to jog, and eventually you become strong enough to run ten miles.

Effective managing is a lot like being in good physical shape: the hard part is getting in the habit of doing it every day no matter what obstacles come up. So stop letting yourself off the hook. Stay in touch with your true priorities. Make yourself do it every day, as if your health depended on it.

Start by setting aside one hour every day as your sacrosanct time for managing. During that hour, do not fight fires. Use that hour for managing up front, before anything goes right, wrong, or average. That one hour every day is just for staying in shape—just for taking a walk.

What if you don't have much experience? You have to start somewhere.

What if you don't enjoy managing people in a hands-on manner? Do it anyway.

What if you don't think that you are skilled at managing? Practice, practice, practice until you become good at it.

What if it makes you uncomfortable? Live with the discomfort; the more you manage people, the more comfortable you will become.

Taking those first steps toward effective managing takes discipline and guts. New behaviors, no matter how good they are, often don't feel comfortable until they become habits. It is likely that you will feel the loss of your old comfortable habits, of your former role in the workplace, and of your current relationships with your employees. The transition period will be difficult and painful. But if you do it right, it is good pain. Like exercise pain, it makes you stronger. After you've built more effective management habits, you'll still have to deal with unexpected problems, but they won't be the kinds of problems that could have been avoided. And you'll still have to face plenty of difficult challenges when managing your employees—the occasional ten-mile run. But you'll be in such good shape that you'll be able to handle it effectively with confidence and skill.

Yes, it will be difficult, but it works: guts, discipline, and one hour a day.

The Second Person You Need to Manage Every Day Is Everyone Else

In an ideal world, you would talk with every single person—reviewing his work and setting him up for success—who calls you his boss every single day. You would take that management walk every day with every person.

Some managers favor team meetings instead of daily one-on-one talks, but team meetings are no substitute. When you meet with an employee, and look her in the eye, talk about expectations, ask for an account of her performance, review her work results, or provide feedback, there's no place to hide. In a team meeting, however, it's easy to hide—for both the manager and the employees. Managers often feel more comfortable sharing difficult news or providing feedback to the whole team than talking directly to one person. The problem is, the difficult news or feedback is often aimed at only one or two people. So the rest of the team is confused and insulted. Meanwhile, the very people you are trying to "manage" in that team setting might not even realize that you are talking to them! Managers tell me all the time about that team meeting in which they meant to shine a bright light on Mr. Blue, the employee who has been coming in late and taking too many long breaks. They announce at the meeting, "We have to stop coming in late. And we have to stop taking so many long breaks. Remember, you get two ten-minute breaks—and ten minutes means ten minutes." Most of their employees are sitting there, puzzled: "What is he talking about? I come in early every day, and I hardly ever take breaks." But the one employee the manager is really talking to is looking at her watch thinking, "Come on already. Wrap it up. I've got to take my break."

It's also a whole lot harder to tune in to each employee in a team meeting and focus on that person's work in a way that will be meaningful and helpful. Often, team meetings feel pro forma and include lots of discussion about things that most of the people in the room don't need to know and don't care about. Meanwhile, details critical to one employee or another are inevitably omitted. Sometimes the best things to come out of a team meeting are the spontaneous one-on-one huddles that typically follow the meeting, because the meeting has made it clear that they are necessary.

Team meetings do have a place in good management, of course. Team meetings are ideal when you need to share information that is relevant to the whole team. And they are often necessary when many people are working interdependently and might benefit from listening to what others are doing, what issues are coming up in their projects, and so on. Yes, team meetings have their place. Just don't fool yourself: the team meeting is a totally different animal from the one-on-one conversation.

How Can You Manage Sixteen or Sixty People Every Day?

Managerial spans of control have gotten wider and wider, and, thus, most managers are responsible for too many people. Without a doubt, this has contributed to the undermanagement epidemic. Faced with managing sixteen, sixty, or even more employees, managers throw their hands up in frustration. They say to me, "How can I possibly talk one-on-one with every single employee, every single day, in just one hour a day?!" Instead, they hide in their offices, complete the required management paperwork, and do little "managing" beyond that. No wonder there is so much "management by special occasion."

If you hide in your office you leave a power vacuum on the day-to-day management front. Then you will run into what I call "the ringleader problem." Ad hoc ringleaders will emerge to fill the vacuum. Often these ringleaders are the squeaky wheels who have good personal relationships with other employees or some brand of charisma. Sometimes they assert their authority and influence in ways that are self-serving and often damaging to the team. They tell people, "Slow down. You're making me look bad." Sometimes they form cliques, bully others, and spread rumors. More often they are simply self-deceived mediocre performers who believe they are high performers. They offer guidance, direction, and support to their coworkers, but they often lead people in the wrong direction.

Do You Have a Chain of Command?

Reality check: Do you really have sixteen or sixty people—or whatever number of people—who directly report to you? Or do you have a "chain of command," that is, employees who are actually managers or supervisors or team leaders who are supposed to be managing some of the other employees in your group?

If you have a chain of command, you must use it effectively. Make a habit of talking to these supervisors or team leaders every day and focus intensely on helping them play the role you need them to play. Teach them how to manage on an ongoing basis, and manage how *they* manage every step of the way. Just as you are working hard to be a great boss, they need to do the same.

If you don't have a chain of command, maybe you should establish one. Although it's best to avoid unnecessary layers of management, if you have sixteen or sixty people, you simply cannot afford to be the only leader on the team. Cultivate and develop high performers who are in your inner circle, who share your priorities and help you keep the team focused on the work at hand. Developing new leaders, even informally, will help you extend your reach: you can use them as temporary project managers and deputize them when you are not available. But don't give anyone management responsibilities of any kind—formal or informal—unless you are prepared to focus on that leader intensely and personally manage that leader's management practices very closely.

You Have to Make Choices Every Day

No matter how many people you are responsible for managing, you have to make choices every day about how you are going to use your dedicated management time.

One very effective manager in a busy hospital taught me this simple reality about making choices: "I have thirty-two nurses that report directly to me and no chain of command. Twelve of those nurses regularly work different shifts than I do and four work in another facility that is twenty miles away. So I have to make choices every day." What does she do? "I concentrate on four or five different nurses each day ... some need more of my time than others. But the meetings are no more than fifteen minutes, and I always have them standing up with my clipboard in hand to make notes. One or two of the nurses I have to meet with every single day, but most of them I speak to only once a week or every other week. At that rate, I talk with everyone pretty frequently. Nobody goes more than two weeks without a stand-up meeting."

What about the nurses working other shifts? "Sometimes I use telephone or e-mail. Sometimes we leave notes for each other. I also make a point of being on site with those nurses at least some of the time. If a nurse works the shift after me, I go out of my way to stick around for a while at the end of my shift once a week or ask that nurse to come in a bit early so we can talk. If a nurse works the shift before me, I'll ask her to stick around for a few minutes after her shift or else I will come in a bit early. When my shift is on the other end of the clock entirely, I'll come in during that nurse's shift, even if I'm not supposed to be working."

What about the nurses working in remote locations? "With the four nurses at our other facility, I have a regularly scheduled phone call every week with each one and these calls are not to be missed. Before each call I send an e-mail saying, 'Here's exactly what we need to discuss ... please be prepared to discuss A, B, C, and D on our call.' Then I make the call and have the conversation and then I send a follow-up e-mail saying, 'This is what we agreed,' complete with a to-do list. I also make a point of driving out to see them once in a while and when I'm there, we don't 'shoot the breeze.' We use that time to really clarify expectations and reinforce the feedback I've been providing."

Some people need more attention than others. Talking to every person every day is not always possible. You have to choose your targets. Just don't make the mistake of choosing the same targets over and over again. Spread out your management time. Some employees may need you more than others, but everybody needs you.

As long as you conduct them on a regular basis, there is no reason to let management conversations become long and convoluted. The goal is to make these one-on-one meetings routine, brief, straight and simple. Once you've gotten into a routine with each person, fifteen minutes should be all you need. Like everything else, it's a moving target. Over time, you'll have to gauge how much time you need to spend with each employee one day as opposed to another, depending upon the person and the work that person is doing.

What if things are not going well with a particular employee? Consider meeting with this person every day for a while. Don't make the mistake of spending hours on tearful inquisitions, indictments, or confessions. Keep these meetings short and consistent. There's a strong chance that things are not working out with an employee because he is not getting enough guidance, direction, and support. Once you spend more time with this person, you are likely to see 90 percent of performance problems disappear as if they were never there in the first place.

What about high performers? Do you really need to spend fifteen minutes every day or even every week with an employee when things are going very well? Maybe you need to meet with that person only every other week. But if you don't spend at least that much time with an employee, then you don't actually know whether things are going well with that person. All you really know is that no problems have come up on your radar screen. So when you think things are going well with an employee, spend those fifteen minutes verifying that things are indeed going as well as you think they are. If in fact they are, then you still need to work with that employee to help make things go even better, to offer her enough positive feedback, to provide the development she needs, and to ensure she is happy so she doesn't think about leaving. High performers need to be managed, too!

You'll be surprised at how much you can get done in fifteen minutes. Take any employee you have not spoken to in detail for a while. Spend fifteen minutes with that person asking probing questions about his work. It is almost always the case that you will find some surprises. You will find things that require adjustment. You'll be darned glad you had that conversation. And you should be in a hurry to have another one, no more than two weeks thereafter.

At fifteen minutes per meeting, you should be able to have four meetings a day in an hour. That's twenty meetings a week, at least. I bet that's a whole lot more than you've been managing lately. Here are a few tips to get you started.

- Concentrate on four or five people a day.

- Make your meetings quick, no more than fifteen minutes.

- Consider holding meetings standing up, with a clipboard in hand (to keep them quick and focused).

- Don't let anybody go more than two weeks without a meeting.

- If you manage people working other shifts, stay late or come in early to meet with them.

- If you manage people in remote locations, communicate via telephone and e-mail regularly and consistently in between one-on-one meetings.

These tactics may not be convenient. I'm sorry, but you are the boss. Inconvenience goes with the territory.

What Should You Talk About?

The fundamental activity of managing is communication. Talk about the work when things are going right, wrong, or average. Maintain an ongoing dialogue with every employee: "Here's what I need from you. What do you need from me?"

You'll have to use your growing knowledge of each person, her tasks and responsibilities, and the overall situation to guide you during each conversation. For each person and on each day, you'll have to decide what to focus on and what to say. The more you do it, the stronger and more informed your judgments will be about what can be done and what cannot, what resources are necessary, what problems may occur, what expectations are reasonable, what goals and deadlines are sufficiently ambitious, and what counts as success versus failure.

Check in regularly to ensure that there are no obstacles in the employee's way that will prevent her from getting lots of work done very well, very fast, all day long. You should ask yourself: Are there problems that haven't been spotted yet? Problems that need to be solved? Resources that need to be obtained? Are there any instructions or goals that are not clear? Has anything happened since we last talked that I should know about? Answer employees' questions as they come up. Get input from your employees throughout the process. Learn from what your employees are learning on the front line. Strategize together. Provide advice, support, motivation, and, yes, even inspiration once in a while.

Get in the Habit of Managing Every Day

I know you are busy. I know your time is limited. You *don't* have enough time. So you *don't* have time *not* to manage.

Dedicate the time to manage every day—at the beginning of the day or at some other time that works for you. Make it a rigorous habit. It's just like exercise. Put in that hour every day. Take that walk every day. It will start to pay off almost immediately. You'll start getting in shape. Things will go better.

Yes, you may have weak moments, weak days, weak weeks, even weak months. As hard as you try, you will sometimes drop the ball. Your employees will notice. And it will be really hard to start managing again after being disengaged for some period of time. After all, you are human. So what do you do when you slip back into your old undermanagement habits? First, try to bounce back sooner rather than later. One mistake managers make is they feel so guilty and sheepish after going through a rough patch that they remain disengaged much longer than they should. If you've been disengaged, have fallen out of your hands-on routine, or are off schedule, the only thing to do is to get back on schedule and into your routine as fast as possible. It's okay to acknowledge your failure in your discussions with your employees. Promise to do better.

Get back to work and do better.

CHAPTER 3

Learn to Talk Like a Performance Coach

You spend plenty of time talking with your employees, right? You talk, talk, talk about everything under the sun. "How was your weekend? How was your kid's birthday party? Did you watch that TV show?" You probably talk about personal matters in order to build a friendly rapport with them. But that approach bleeds into your management relationship, so when the subject matter turns to work, you tend to soft-pedal your authority. When you have a difficult task that you must press upon an employee, or, even worse, there is a problem that you must address with him or her, you suddenly shift gears and start talking seriously, urgently, and sometimes heatedly about the work. That's when the employee is likely to say, "Hey, I thought we were friends!?!" And all the rapport goes out the window.

This is what I call the "Jekyll and Hyde" problem. If you do all of your rapport building with employees by talking about personal matters as if you are personal friends, then, when the conversation turns serious—as it always does—you have to adopt a whole different personality. You go from being Mr. Nice Guy Friend to Mr. Jerk Boss, at least until the dust settles and you can go back to being Mr. Friend again. The problem is that Mr. Friend starts feeling like a fake and Mr. Boss struggles for legitimacy.

Talk, Talk, Talk about the Work

If you want to be Mr. Friend to your employees, go out for a beer with them after work. But *at* work, you need to be the boss. Your role is keeping everybody focused on the work and each person performing at her best every day. The good news is that the best way to build rapport with your employees is actually by talking about the work. Work is what you have in common; in fact, it's the reason you have a relationship at all. When you build rapport by talking about work, you are making conflict less likely and, at the same time, building rapport that will survive conflict when it does occur. So talk about the work that's been done and the work that needs to be done. Talk about avoiding pitfalls, finding shortcuts, making sure resources are available. Talk about goals, deadlines, guidelines, and specifications. Talk, talk, talk about the work. Things will go much better.

How Do the Most Effective Managers Talk?

Many managers tell me, "I'm not a natural leader. I'm an ____." (You fill in the blank: accountant, engineer, doctor, etc.) They say, "I don't really enjoy managing. It involves a lot of difficult conversations." What these managers are really saying is that they don't know how to talk to their employees about the work in an effective way.

Only the rarest of managers has that special brand of charisma, contagious passion, and infectious enthusiasm that inspires and motivates people. What about the rest of us? You may not be able to learn how to develop charisma, but you can learn to talk about the work in a straightforward and effective manner. You can learn to say the right words to your employees at the right time in the right way.

The most effective managers have a special way of talking. They adopt a special posture, demeanor, and tone. They have a way of talking that is both authoritative and sympathetic; both demanding and supportive; both disciplined and patient. It is a way of talking that is neither Mr. Friend nor Mr. Boss, but rather nearly exactly in the middle. This special way of talking looks a lot like performance coaching.

"I've never had a great coach," managers sometimes tell me, "so I don't know what coaching sounds like." I can describe it for you: The voice of performance coaching is steady and persistent, relentlessly methodical and hands-on, enthusiastic and pushy. It is the constant banter of focus, improvement, and accountability. Think about the best boss you ever had, or the best teacher or camp counselor or pastor. Hear the sound of her voice, her tone, her honesty, her clarity. Remember the impact she had on you.

When I think about performance coaching, I think of Frank Gorman—the greatest teacher I have ever known and the über-coach. As long as I've known him, Frank has been focused on one thing: karate. He happens to have that special charisma, passion, and enthusiasm that characterizes strong leaders. He is a master at getting people to share his focus, and work intensely on one short-term goal for hours on end without even considering a break in the action. How does he do that?

"The only thing that matters is your thumbs," Frank would tell me over and over again for weeks. "Pull in your thumbs; press them hard against your palms, so hard the tendons in your forearms raise up." Here I would be sweating and straining from physical exhaustion, trying to keep my eyes straight ahead, chin down, shoulders back, elbows in, back straight, hips square, feet pressed into the floor and twisting to tighten the leg muscles. And Frank Gorman would be yelling, somehow in a whisper, "Your thumbs; pull in your thumbs ... The only thing that matters is your thumbs."

Then one day, the only thing that mattered was ... something else: my eyes, my chin, my shoulders, and so on and so on. Finally, some years ago, I asked, "How can my thumbs be the only thing that matters in karate? How can that be, when what matters changes all the time: It's always something different!" Frank smiled and said, "Nobody can learn karate in a day or a year. All we have is today. What can I teach you right now? What can you focus on right now? What can you improve right now? The only thing that matters is *what we are doing here right now.*"

What I learned from Frank is that the unyielding force of your persistent voice leaves the person you are coaching with no choice other than to focus acutely on whatever he or she is doing right now. For those being coached this way, the demands are intense, but the payoff is incredible. When you coach people to success in this manner, they have no choice but to get "into" their work because you, like few others in their lives, require them to be great. You remind them to be purposeful about every single detail. You help them build their skills one day at a time. From focusing, they learn focus itself. They become black belts at whatever they do. Perhaps long after they work for you, they will carry your voice of constant feedback in their heads: "The only thing that matters is what we are doing here right now."

Obviously, some people have more natural talent than others when it comes to coaching. But talking like a coach is something that can be learned. Should you imitate that performance coach from your past? Yes. Try it out. It's a great place to start. Over time, you'll develop your own style.

You Don't Have to Holler, "Rah! Rah!"

Sometimes managers worry that if they try to talk like a performance coach, they just won't seem genuine, that they'll sound contrived. As one senior manager in a software firm put it, "There's no way I'm going around the office hollering, 'Rah! Rah!' I'm just not the coaching type."

But performance coaching has very little to do with hollering, "Rah! Rah!" around the office. It's simply a technique. And here's the really good news: In order to be effective, coaching simply cannot be contrived. It must be totally genuine. Often it is so genuine that you don't even realize you are doing it.

That's how I responded to this software manager. Then I asked him to recall some of his best management interactions over the years. As he began describing some of his management high points, a smile slowly crossed his face. What do you know? His descriptions sounded a lot like performance coaching: "I was really thinking about the person as an individual. Where was he coming from? I was trying really hard to focus on the performance, not the person. I was choosing my words so carefully. I wanted to make it very clear exactly what I already knew about the situation and what I didn't know. I was asking questions, but mostly pushing toward some concrete next steps. We were right in the middle of this project, so I made really sure to spell out exactly what he had done right and exactly what was done wrong. Then we worked out a detailed plan of next steps and I kept following up to check in on those next steps, one by one, until they were done."

That is exactly how a performance coach talks:

- Tune in to the individual you are coaching.

- Focus on specific instances of individual performance.

- Describe the employee's performance honestly and vividly.

- Develop concrete next steps.

Don't Wait for Problems to Start Coaching

Early on in our work with managers, we learned that some managers are simply masterful at coaching, but most were not so great at it. Yet whether managers were good or bad at it, it became clear that when it comes to managing people, so much of the real action takes place during these coaching conversations.

The problem is that most managers only coach employees when they encounter a recurring performance problem, such as missed deadlines or poor work quality, or a behavior issue, such as a bad attitude toward customers or coworkers. When it starts to look like a problem isn't going away, that's when the manager decides to bring the employee into her office and coach the employee: "There is a problem with your performance, and we need to have some sessions until 'we' coach you out of this problem."

By this point, there are probably some bad feelings. The manager might be thinking, "What is your problem?!" And the employee might think, "Gee, why didn't you talk to me about this sooner?" Often the only next steps the manager can articulate amount to, "Don't do this again." This leaves both the manager and the employee wondering when the problem will recur. Don't forget, if this is a recurring problem, that's probably because the employee either doesn't know what steps to follow to avoid the problem or else he has gotten into one or more bad habits that cause the problem to recur.

By the time a problem is recurring, it is too late to start coaching. The time to coach an employee is in advance so you can set her up for success. For example, if you have an employee who chronically misses deadlines, don't wait until she misses the deadline to coach her. Start coaching her when the deadline is first set. Help her establish intermediate benchmarks, such as deadlines along the way. Every step of the way, help the employee make a plan for completing those intermediate deadlines. And check in with the employee frequently. Talk through the accomplishment of each step in advance. Do that and 99 percent of the time that employee is going to start meeting her deadlines.

Stop coaching employees when problems develop; coach employees when they are doing great or doing just okay. Coach

people every step of the way and help them develop good habits
before they ever have a chance to develop bad ones.

Get Extraordinary Performance out of Ordinary People

I've had the tremendous honor of working with many leaders in
the United States Armed Forces over the years. One of the stun-
ning things about the military is its remarkable ability to teach
huge numbers of young and relatively inexperienced people to
be extremely effective leaders. Take the Marine Corps, for example. With a one-to-nine ratio of officers to enlisted people,
the Marine Corps is forced to depend a great deal on enlisted
leaders. At any given time, nearly one out of eight marines is a
corporal in charge of a fire team of three marines. The Marine
Corps transforms ordinary nineteen-year-olds into effective
leaders all day, every day. How do they do that?

New recruits are coached aggressively from day one. Every
day, all day long, for thirteen weeks in boot camp, new marines
are told exactly what to do and how to do it; they are monitored,
measured, and documented every step of the way. Problems are
not tolerated, and even the least reward must be earned through
hard work. After boot camp, marines are still coached aggressively, thoroughly, and thoughtfully all day, every day.

When it comes to building new enlisted leaders, like everything else they do, the Marine Corps is painfully methodical.
Marines are trained in the techniques of performance coaching before they ascend to the role of fire-team leader. They are
taught to tune in to each individual Marine, give constant feed-

back on his performance, and provide step-by-step instruction to improve it. The new fire-team leader takes full responsibility for that team, knows exactly who is doing what, where, why, when, and how. He spells out expectations; monitors, measures, and documents his Marines' performance; and addresses problems as they come up. The fire-team leader takes care of his marines. As a result, the average Marine fire-team leader is a better manager at age nineteen than most senior executives with decades of experience.

"We have to get extraordinary performance out of ordinary people," one Marine officer told me. "The only way to do that is to squeeze that out of every single person every single day through relentless in-your-face leadership all the way down to the lowest level."

They call it relentless in-your-face leadership. I call it performance coaching. Learn to talk like a performance coach and squeeze extraordinary performance out of every person.

CHAPTER 4

Take It One Person at a Time

Y ou look around the table at your monthly staff meeting and survey the members of your team. It's amazing how different they all are: Sam is a creative type. Mary is analytical. Joe is outgoing. Chris is shy. Harold is highly skilled, but easily distracted. Bob is really enthusiastic, but doesn't have the experience to match. Rita is totally focused, but not always on the right things. Juanita is a perfectionist, and takes forever to finish anything. As each employee takes a turn giving a status report on his individual work, you pay especially close attention because you will be preparing annual performance evaluations for every one of them soon. Most of the team is doing fine. Mary and Joe are doing especially great as usual. But Chris and Harold are struggling.

Every employee is different, yet most managers take roughly the same approach to managing every person in their group. Whatever technique they use to manage—weekly reports, monthly team meetings, or annual reviews—it is rarely calibrated to the individuals being managed. Instead, it is based on prevailing practices in the organization and the manager's own style. This is what I call "one-size-fits-all" management. Whatever the one-size-fits-all approach may be in any given case, it works fine for some employees but not so well for others. Those who respond well to it appear to be high performers, while those who respond poorly appear to be low performers. Instead of managing every person to success, the boss manages everyone the same regardless of each person's needs—let the chips fall where they may.

But would you take the same approach to maintaining a car as you would to a toaster? Of course not; you would calibrate your care and maintenance to the specifications of the machine. So why not calibrate your approach to managing based on what works best for each employee? Every person is different. Deal with it.

Figure Out What Works with Each Employee

All of your employees come to work with different levels of ability and skill: different backgrounds, personalities, styles, ways of communicating, work habits, and motivations. Some of them need more guidance than others. One employee needs details spelled out, while another has the details memorized. One responds best if you ask questions, while another prefers you tell him all the answers. Some need lots of reminders, while others need you to check in just once a week. The only way to cope with the incredible diversity among your employees is to figure out what works with each person and then customize your management style accordingly.

Customize Your Management

I'm not suggesting that you cater to the whims of each employee. But whims are not *all* bad. When you know the whims of an employee, you know what that person wants and you learn how to gain leverage with him. Am I saying "coddle employees"? No. Still, if an employee needs you to hold his hand and spoon-feed him assignments, you need to know that. In the end, you need to decide whether you are willing to do that for this employee, but don't pretend he doesn't need it. Finally, I'm not suggesting that you ask each employee how he wants to be managed. What an employee wants from you is not always the same as what he needs. For example, try asking a stubborn low performer if he wants your feedback on his performance. He'll likely say, "Feedback? None for me, thanks." Often employees think that they know what they want from you, but in fact they often don't know what they want until they get it and it starts working.

The only way to learn what really works with each employee is to get in there and start managing. Those one-on-one conversations are the path inside. When you start having individual meetings with each person, the differences between your employees will jump right out at you. As you talk with each person face-to-face, try to tune in to that person and adjust your approach this way and that, just as you adjust the tuner on a radio. Be aware of how you are changing your approach and observe carefully the effects of each change on each person and her performance. And remember, you'll have to keep making adjustments constantly because people change and grow over time.

The best way to keep fine-tuning your approach to each person is to continually ask yourself six key questions about each employee:

- Who is this person at work?

- Why do I need to manage this person?

- What do I need to talk about with this person?

- How should I talk with this person?

- Where should I talk with this person?

- When should I talk with this person?

Together, these six questions make up one of the most powerful management tools I know of—I call it the "customizing" lens. If you become obsessed with asking and answering these questions, you won't be able to avoid customizing your approach with each person. Start asking and answering these questions and you'll see what I mean.

Who Is This Person at Work?

Don't worry: You don't need to ask yourself who this person is deep inside—what her mind and spirit are like, or what her inner motivations are. In fact, you shouldn't try. You are not qualified to do so, unless you are trained in counseling or you have a special sixth sense. Focus on figuring out the "self" this employee brings to work. That will be plenty.

Assess this person's basic strengths and weaknesses as an employee. Consider his tasks and responsibilities. What is the nature of the work he handles? Assess his performance record. Is this one of your high performers, average workers, or low performers? Is he productive? Does he do high-quality work? Think about his work background and likely career future. How long has he been working here? How long is he likely to stay? Consider his social role in your workplace. Is he high energy or low? An enthusiast or a naysayer? Is he well liked? Talkative? Do other employees hold him in high regard or low?

Often managers ask me, "How much do I need to know about what's going on in an employee's personal life?" My answer: You need to know enough to be polite. Know that an employee has two kids. It would be a nice gesture if you remember roughly how old the kids are. It would be extra nice if you remember the kids' names. But you really don't need to remember their birthdays or keep their pictures in your wallet.

You should understand how an employee's personal life bears on his role at work. Does his home life affect his schedule? Energy level? Concentration? And so on. The truth is that lots of employees leave their personal issues at home ... but not everybody does.

Not long ago, I was debriefing with a senior executive of a hotel company after spending the day training a group of her managers. She immediately asked me what I thought about the head of housekeeping, a twentysomething woman who had obviously not been at her best during my seminar. I'll call her Alice. As the head of housekeeping, Alice was supposed to be in charge of a team of eight housekeeping managers.

For about eight hours that day, I had watched Alice stare off into space. Though she hardly participated in the seminar, when she did speak, she uttered incoherent non sequiturs in a low unclear voice, and then wandered off to the ladies' room. What did I think about Alice? "If her behavior at work is anything like her behavior in the seminar," I told the executive, "I would be very worried about the housekeeping department." That's when the executive told me that Alice had some serious family problems at home. These problems, apparently, happened on an on-again, off-again basis. When the problems went away, Alice was one of their best employees and an especially conscientious manager. But whenever the problems returned, Alice was a mess. She arrived late and left early and disappeared for hours in the middle of the day. She was distracted and had low energy and could barely communicate.

"I'm amazed she made it all the way through your seminar," Alice's boss told me. "We all feel sorry for her. A couple of years ago, I helped her get some counseling through employee services, which she really appreciated. Things were better for a while ... and then things got worse again ... and then they got better ... and now things are worse again." This had been going on for years. Then I got the big punch line: "It's none of my business what Alice does in her personal life, right? I can't fire her because she's having problems at home, right?"

It's clarifying to reframe this very complicated issue in clear and simple terms: the question is not whether this person is having troubles at home, but rather, "Who is this person at work?" At work, Alice was highly inconsistent. She went through distinct periods as a high performer and distinct periods as a low performer. What should Alice's boss do? One of the options, I suggested, was to manage Alice like a high performer when she's up and like a low performer when she is down. Managing Alice when she's low would take tremendous effort, and her manager might not be able to manage Alice to the level the company needs her to perform at—especially since she's a manager herself. In the end, the executive felt that she couldn't have a manager whose performance was so inconsistent, especially when her performance would decrease so markedly when troubles at home intensified. The next day, she made the decision to fire Alice, not because Alice was going through problems at home, but because of who she was at work.

Maybe you are thinking, "Alice is a special case." *Every* employee is a special case. If you don't know what makes one of your employees a special case, you better find out. Keep asking yourself: "Who is this person at work?"

- Assess each employee's basic strengths and weaknesses.

- Consider the role each person plays in your workplace.

- Know how issues at home bear on an employee's role at work.

- Manage the self each employee brings to work.

Why Do I Need to Manage This Person?

The key to answering this question is to have a clear understanding of your goals for managing each person and what you need from her. Do you need this person to do more work? Better work? Faster work? To change some behavior? With some people, if you don't talk to them every day about their to-do list, they might not do any work. With others, if you don't talk through with them exactly how to do a particular task, they might do it wrong. With one employee, if you don't point out the shortcuts, he'll take forever.

Whatever your reasons for managing employees, don't make the mistake of thinking that some are so talented, skilled, and motivated that you don't need to manage them at all. Even superstars must be managed. Like everyone else, superstars have bad days, sometimes go in the wrong direction, and have lapses in judgment or integrity. Even superstars need guidance, direction, support, and encouragement. They need to be challenged and developed. What is more, superstars often want to know that someone is keeping track of their great work and looking for ways to reward them.

Sometimes managers tell me, "This superstar is different. She is so talented, skilled, and motivated that I have nothing to offer her." If that's truly the case, it doesn't mean the person doesn't need a boss. It just means that maybe *you* shouldn't be the person's boss. If that's the case, then perhaps you should promote her, move her to a boss who does have something to offer her, or change your relationship with her so that you work together as partners or collaborators. More often, what managers are really saying is "This person is so talented, skilled, and motivated that she is able to handle more responsibility than most. She can make her own project plans; she gets lots of work done very well, very fast, all day, every day; she doesn't cause problems; she learns quickly and steadily; she has great relationship skills; she understands the big picture; she is a great critical thinker; and she takes exactly the right amount of initiative without overstepping. How do I deal with that?"

You need to manage this superstar because she challenges you in ways that you don't expect. She forces you to stay on your toes and think on your feet. You need to check in regularly to make sure that things are going as well as you think, ask her for regular reports on her projects and responsibilities. Regardless of her talents, you need to verify that the work is getting done. Most of all, you need to manage this superstar so that you can make sure she is getting her needs met and isn't going to start looking for another job. Go out of your way to ask her regularly, "What do you need from me?" Try hard to reward her generously for her great work. And count yourself lucky.

Remember, every employee needs to be managed. If you don't know why one of your employees needs to be managed, you better figure it out:

- Clarify your goals with each person. What do *you* need from this person?

- Keep in mind what might go wrong if you don't manage this person.

- Pay attention: The reasons for managing each person will change over time.

What Do I Need to Talk about with This Person?

Once you figure out why you need to manage a person, you are well on your way to knowing what you need to talk to that person about.

Of course, you need to talk about the work with every employee. But what details should you focus on with each employee? Should you talk to this person about big-picture strategy or, rather, go over his to-do list for the day? Should you review standard procedures for each task or talk about ways to be creative with those tasks? What you talk about with any employee, ultimately, should be determined by what you want that employee to do in the immediate future. If you want the person to do more work, then talk about the number of items on his to-do list each day. If you need her to work faster, talk about how long each item on the to-do list is going to take and figure out what's taking so long. If you want her to quit, then you need to tell her, incessantly, all the things that are not going well. If you want the person to never quit, then talk about whether she is happy, has what she needs, or wants something that she is not getting. If you want the person to change some behavior, then talk in detail about exactly how you want him to behave.

A while back, the manager of an audiology clinic told me about his receptionist—I'll call him Chris—who seemed to have a hopeless performance problem. Chris was efficient at opening the clinic on time in the morning, answering the phone, and dealing with patients in the office. But he neglected to open the mail every day and file it as he was supposed to. As a result, other people in the office would pick through the mail each day to find items addressed to them, and the rest of the mail, mostly paperwork that needed to be filed, would pile up on Chris's desk. The manager told me, "I actually saw Chris using a dustpan to scoop up excess mail that had fallen onto the floor … I watched him dump it right back on the pile on his desk!"

On top of this, whenever patients called to check if their hearing aids were ready, Chris would answer yes or no—but his answers were not based on accurate information about whether the hearing aids were in fact ready. "Frankly, I have no idea how he decides whether to say yes or no," Chris's manager told me. "I think he's just winging it. Usually, he just says no and they call back again. The real problem is when he says yes. About half the time he's right, I think by chance. But the other half of the time, people come in to pick up their hearing aid and it's not ready. Sometimes they have driven quite a way and often they are older people. They complain bitterly. I've talked to Chris about this over and over again. I talk with him about it every time it happens. But it always happens again."

The manager wanted to know, "Do I need to tell Chris, 'Each morning, print out the status list of hearing aids on order. Keep it by your desk. When a patient calls to see if her hearing aid is ready, check the list. If it's ready, say yes. If it's not ready, check the delivery date on the list and ask her to call back on that day.' Do I really need to spell it out that much for him?" My answer: When you don't spell it out for Chris, he gets it wrong. So, yes. Spell it out for him, every day if necessary. Also spell out how he needs to distribute the mail every day. Turn that big pile of mail on his desk into a project. Give him a clear deadline. Break it down into smaller goals with a series of deadlines if you want. Give him precise instructions. If you have time, go through some of the pile with him so that you can see if he knows how to file the paperwork properly. If he doesn't, you can use this project to instruct him.

Several weeks later, I heard from this manager with an update about Chris: "Sure enough. All I had to do was tell him! I reminded him every day for a while. Now when I walk by Chris's desk in the morning, he waves the [hearing aid] status list at me with a smile and says, 'And don't worry, I won't forget the mail today.'" Amazing!

With every employee, keep asking yourself: "What do I need to talk about today?"

- Talk about the work.

- Focus on what you want the employee to do in the immediate future.

- Decide whether you should talk about the big picture or all the minor details.

- For some employees, breaking things down and spelling them out can make the difference between high performance and low performance.

How Should I Talk with This Person?

How should you talk about the work with each person? Some employees respond best if you ask questions. Others prefer that you just take the lead and do most of the talking. Some employees respond best if you take an even-measured tone and stick to the facts alone—the auditor style. Some respond best if you talk with more feeling—the older-sibling style. Some employees respond best if you pepper them with difficult leading questions—the cross-examining-attorney style. Some employees respond best to effusive enthusiasm—the cheerleader style. Some employees respond best to worry and fear and urgency—the Chicken Little style.

Keep in mind that what motivates each person is different, too. Some employees are enthusiasts and you need to tap their enthusiasm. Others crave inspiration. Some employees seek approval. Others are working to put food on the table. Some employees are all about the work. Others are all about the money. Some throw their whole identity into work and work into their identity. Others need to be reminded constantly where they are and what they are supposed to be doing and why.

How you manage is partly a matter of tone and style. Of course, you don't want to try too hard at a style that doesn't fit you. Nor are you looking for a tone and style that makes the employee comfortable, or makes you comfortable. Comfort is not the issue here. You are looking for the right tone and style to motivate each employee best and get your point across un-equivocally. Ultimately, this question is about choosing the best tools and techniques for communicating with each employee on a day-to-day basis. Some employees are more challenging to communicate with than others.

Nowadays, it is not uncommon for managers to be struggling to manage employees with whom they have a real language barrier—the manager and the employee actually do not speak the same language. Now *that* is a communication challenge. What tools and techniques can possibly solve that one? How are you going to manage this person and make sure he understands exactly what you need him to do and how?

One manager in a landscaping business who deals with this problem every day suggests the following techniques: "You need to have someone on the crew who speaks both languages ... you need a translator." Second, teach and learn. "Most of the guys on the crew are Spanish speaking. Over the years, I've learned a little bit of Spanish, some key terms anyway ... and most of the guys start learning some English after a while." At least you can start to build up some shared vocabulary, maybe a combination of both languages that you can use to communicate what needs to be done and how. This manager explained, "Believe it or not, we also use our own sign language. I point a lot. Sometimes I do a little demonstration and have the employee imitate me. I do a lot of thumbs-up and thumbs-down, too."

Another common technique is creating checklists and other written tools in both languages. That way, managers can actually point to items on the checklist and the manager and employee both know what they mean. This also helps the manager and employee learn key terms in each other's language and gradually start talking about the checklists.

Keep asking yourself: "How do I need to talk to this person?"

- Think about what motivates this person.

- Figure out what tone and style work best.

- Most employees respond best to verbal communication supported by visual aids in writing.

- Choose the right communication tools and techniques for each person.

Where Should I Talk with This Person?

Whether it's your office or some other obvious place to meet, it's best to choose a place that works and then make a habit of meeting there. That space will become the physical scene in which your management relationship with that person develops. Choose it well.

If your employees work in remote locations, you should rely primarily on a rigorous protocol of telephone calls and e-mails. But if you work in the same location with your employee, the best place to meet might be on neutral ground. One manager told me that he and his employees are on their feet all the time and there is no obvious place to meet, so he takes employees into the stairwell for their quick talks. Restaurant folks often tell me that they take employees to a booth in the back for their one-on-one meetings. Factory workers often step away from the machinery so they can hear. Soldiers sometimes huddle behind a large rock. My own favorite venue for meetings is taking a walk (as anyone who has come to meet with me can attest!); just make sure you and your employee bring along a pad and pen so you can write stuff down.

Keep asking yourself: "Where do I need to manage this person?"

- Choose a place that works for you and your employee.

- Try to meet in that same place every week.

- Rely on the telephone and e-mail to communicate with employees in remote locations.

When Should I Talk with This Person?

When you are considering what days and times to meet each employee, you are often limited by your schedules.

Sometimes the time you meet is dictated completely by logistics. For example, if an employee works a different shift than you do, she may need to come in a little early or you might need to stay late to meet her. Sometimes the best time to meet is a matter of moods. Maybe you have an employee who gets a slow start in the morning (or maybe *you* get a slow start), and so you decide it's best to meet with that person just before lunch instead of first thing in the morning.

Sometimes the best time might be indicated by a performance issue. Let's say you have an employee who is chronically late to work. Some managers try to deal with that problem by scheduling early morning meetings. I happen to think that if you want to help an employee arrive on time to work, the best time to meet with that employee is at the end of the day, just before that person leaves. The next item on that person's to-do list will be coming in to work—which is exactly what you want to focus on at the end of your meeting: "I want to remind you that we start at 8:00 a.m. in this office. How long does it take you to get to work? Twenty minutes? Okay. How long does it take you to get ready in the morning? Thirty minutes? Okay. So what time do you normally get up in the morning? Seven thirty? Aha! That's the problem. You need to start getting up at 7:00! Do you want me to call you in the morning and give you a wake-up call?" Have that conversation a few times at the end of the day, before the employee leaves, and I promise you that employee is likely to start coming to work on time.

One manager who runs a beer distributorship told me he tried this technique with one chronically late employee. "Every time she was late, she had told me that she missed the bus ... this time I waited until the end of the day. I asked her what bus she normally takes. She told me the 8:40 a.m. bus. I asked her if there was an earlier bus. She said there was an 8:20 and an 8:00. So I asked her to please try to catch the 8:00 or the 8:20 bus. Then I reminded her every day for a week on her way out the door, 'Please try to catch the 8:00 or the 8:20 bus tomorrow morning, okay?' She has never been late again."

But perhaps a tougher question than what time of day is best to meet with an employee is *how often to meet with each employee.*

First, keep this in mind: Most of your employees need to talk with you about their work a lot more often than you would guess, and much more often than they currently do. I always urge managers to force themselves to meet more often than they think necessary, until they know exactly what the person is doing—where, when, why, and how. Over time, you will probably be able to step back a bit and meet less often.

Second, most people need to talk with you more when they are new to a job, or working on a new task or project, and then less over time. But remember that it's a moving target. You'll have to start meeting more often again if the employee gets a new task, responsibility, or project; if the employee slows down, starts missing details, or develops a behavior issue. As things improve, you can probably step back again and meet less often.

Most self-starting high performers probably don't need to meet with you every day. If one of your high performers starts taking over your one-on-one meetings, laying out her to-do list for the week, including step-by-step plans, and then offering you memos summarizing these presentations, that is usually an indication that you can step back even a little bit more.

But employees who don't perform as well might require one-on-one meetings much more frequently—maybe every single day as they come in the door. I call this coaching employees into their roles: "Okay, Mr. Green, you're going to be here for five hours, right? Here's what I want you to do: A, B, C, and D. Okay? Let's go through A ... and through B ... and so on. Here's a checklist. Are you ready?"

That conversation—coaching an employee into her role— takes five to fifteen minutes. If you have employees who need a lot of coaching and guidance, try coaching them into their roles every time they walk in the door. Watch their performance improve radically in miracle time.

For some employees, even that's not enough. Particularly low performers might need to be coached twice or three times a day, or they slow down and lose focus. But at what point do you say enough? Deciding that an employee requires so much of your management time that it's just not worth it is a tough business call. You have to consider whether this employee is much less able, skilled, and motivated than other employees that you could hire from your available labor pool. Sometimes, depending on the job and the labor available for it, the only way you are going to get high performance consistently is if you commit to high-intensity management—twice, three times, four times a day. But sometimes the answer is clear: "No way! I'm paying this person too much and this job is too high level to justify the kind of management time this person requires."

Keep asking yourself: "When do I need to manage this person?"

What days and times work best?

- Sometimes the time is dictated by logistics.

- The best time might depend upon your and your employees' typical mood schedules.

- The best time might be indicated by a performance issue.

How often?

- Most people need to talk with you a lot more than you would guess.

- Most need to talk more when they are working on something new.

- Force yourself to meet more often than you think necessary for a while.

- Over time, you will probably step back a bit and meet less often.

Is it worth it? Do the math for yourself.

The Manager's Landscape

Try creating for yourself what I call a "manager's landscape." Write down these questions across the top of a piece of paper: Who? Why? What? How? Where? When? In the first column— under "Who?"—list each person you manage and make a few notes about what you know or think you know about each of them. Then write notes for each employee under the "Why?" "What?" "How?" "Where?" and "When?" columns. If you lay out all this information on one page, you have before you an instant landscape of the management challenge you face. On that page is your world as a manager. Remember, circumstances change. People change. That means you have to revisit these questions frequently and revise and adjust your manager's landscape on a regular basis.

Your goal as a manager is to help each person grow and develop. You *want* the answers to these questions to change. Who? You want this person to become a high performer who is really into the work. Why? You want this person to become so good at her job and so valuable that you can talk strategy and big picture, brainstorm great ideas, encourage her to take on more responsibilities, and help her meet more of her needs so she will never quit. What? You want this person to get so good at her job that in your coaching sessions you discuss her plan for her tasks, updates on her progress, ways she can add even more value, and how she can earn even more rewards. How? You want this person to become so competent and confident that you can just sit back and listen. Where? Maybe the person is so successful that she gets her own office and you can start meeting there. When? You want this person to become so good at managing herself that you need to check in only once a week to make sure things are going as well as you think.

Never stop asking yourself and answering these questions.

CHAPTER 5

Make Accountability a Real Process

You just returned from your company's annual management conference, where the theme was accountability. There were a lot of speeches from senior executives and a few outside experts: "Every one of you is accountable for your actions!" said one. "Hold each other accountable!" implored another. And so on. You returned from the conference with your new "accountability" coffee mug and found an e-mail in your in-box from your boss, reminding you that "your job is to hold your people accountable."

Accountability is the new watchword in just about every business. But what does it really mean?

Accountability means having to answer for one's actions. The idea is compelling: if an employee knows that she will have to explain her actions to another person and that her actions will be rewarded or punished accordingly, typically that person will make an effort to act "better." When business leaders chant the slogan "accountability," what they are trying to do is spread the following message to employees: behave knowing in advance that you will have to explain yourself and that your actions will have consequences.

Tie Real Consequences to Employee Performance

In order to make accountability work, it's not enough to chant the slogan around the office and hope people get it.

First, accountability works only as a management tool if the employee knows *in advance* that she will have to answer for her actions. If you tell an employee that she is accountable for her actions *after* she has taken action, it won't affect that person's behavior. Likewise, if you punish a person for her poor performance—without having told her in advance that her actions would be attached to punishments and rewards—it's too late to affect behavior in that instance.

Second, employees must trust and believe that there is a fair and accurate process for keeping track of their actions and tying their behavior to real consequences. Let me show you: What would be the first thing you would want to know if your boss came in tomorrow morning and said, "Today, I am really going to hold you accountable. If you do a great job today, I am going to give you a $1,000 bonus. If you do an average job, you get to keep your job. If you do a bad job today, you are fired." The first thing you'd want to know is exactly what a great job, an average job, and a bad job look like today. Right? After all, if you are going to be held accountable for your actions and there are going to be consequences for them, you would want to know exactly what is expected and required of you. You'd also want to know that someone is keeping a close eye on you all day so that they don't miss it when you do a great job. And, finally, you'd want to ensure that your performance will be measured based on those expectations and requirements that were spelled out up front—and on nothing else.

You need a fair and accurate process for tying real consequences to each employee's real concrete actions. What does that process look like?

- Spell out expectations in advance in vivid terms.

- Track employee performance every step of the way.

- Follow through with real consequences based on whether the employee's actual performance meets those expectations or not.

This process cannot be done once or twice a year, during formal performance evaluations. The process of creating real accountability has to be done up close and often. In the real world, however, you will encounter many complications that make it nearly impossible to maintain an airtight process linking individual actions to consequences. Don't let those complications become excuses for not practicing real accountability. You can hold people accountable, even in a complex world. Consider the seven most common complications that interfere with accountability.

Complication Number One: "I'm waiting for so-and-so or such-and-such."

Sometimes when you ask an employee to account for her actions, she will start blaming others. Sometimes the employee is quite right to do so. In today's complex world, employees usually have to work closely with other employees and whole other departments, not to mention outsiders like customers and vendors. Some employee may have failed to meet clearly spelled-out expectations, such as a deadline, because she is waiting for another employee to finish some piece of the puzzle before she can complete her task. Managers ask me all the time, "How can I fairly hold my employees accountable if they are legitimately held up by someone else in a whole other department?"

First, focus on the tasks your employee can accomplish on her own, without depending on anyone else. You have to accurately define all the steps she can and should take leading up to the point where she has to rely on someone else. Then evaluate how well she accomplished those tasks.

Second, consider how your employee is handling the people she depends upon to accomplish her tasks. You can teach her how to interact more effectively with these people and get more of what she needs from them—and faster.

Finally, if your employee's work is being held up by a coworker or an outsider, spell out exactly what you expect her to do during that waiting period. Help her make a plan to reduce downtime, maintain productivity, and continue moving the project along.

You simply cannot hold an employee accountable for the actions of another person. But you can help your employee better handle these difficult situations and keep the accountability process going by staying focused on concrete actions that are within the employee's control.

Complication Number Two: "Some other work obligations got in the way."

In many organizations, managers often have to manage employees who have more than one boss, and thus have to compete for an employee's time and energy. When you give such an employee an assignment, it's not always clear how many other assignments that employee is juggling or whether an "urgent" assignment from another boss will interfere with completing an assignment on time for you. How can you hold an employee accountable in this case?

A senior manager in a large media company, whom I'll call Phil, had a conversation-stopping answer to this question: "I am absolutely determined to be the manager that employees do not want to disappoint. Everybody knows you don't accept an assignment from me unless you can definitely complete it to my specifications. I am the one who is going to follow up, follow up, follow up. There is nowhere to hide from me. I will come find you; unless you are on your deathbed, you had better have an answer for me." Everybody else in the room was nodding and smiling. It was true: everybody knew that about this manager.

Here's what I learned from Phil and others like him.

- Be the boss who is most engaged and you will be the boss to whom your employees are most responsive. If they know you will follow up, monitor, measure, and document, and insist on accountability, they will always put assignments for you first.

- Be the boss who sets up employees for success and rewards them accordingly. If you do so, the best employees will always want to work for you.

- Be the boss who understands what other projects your employee is juggling for other managers. Ask lots of questions about her other tasks and deadlines. Talk about how your assignment might interfere with her other work. Ask how her other work might interfere with the work you are assigning. Decide together whether she will be able to meet your requirements. Make a plan for how she will respond if any other responsibility interferes with meeting your deadline or meeting your requirements.

- Be the boss who sets higher expectations, standards, and
  requirements. If other managers who are your peers have
  fundamentally different expectations, standards, and requirements for employees, remind your employees regularly and enthusiastically that you are different. Make it a
  point of pride. Let the people on your team appreciate your
  especially high standards and make that part of the esprit
  de corps you all share.

Complication Number Three: "I've been accepting mediocrity for a long time."

Managers often ask me, "How can I suddenly raise my standards and start holding people accountable when I haven't been
doing that all these years?"

To answer that question, I'd like to tell you about a manager
I'll call Debbie. For several years, Debbie ran a research labora-
tory. Most of the researchers she managed worked in the lab
before she got there and were used to working independently
under very little daily supervision. They were not in the habit
of answering to anybody but themselves.

When Debbie first took over the lab, she eased into her role
gently, not wanting to upset the status quo. Four years later, the
lab was running much as it did the day she took over, and things
were not going well. "People pretty much came and went as they
pleased," Debbie told me. "The lab was a mess, literally. Supplies
were not properly labeled and shelved. Safety procedures were not
being followed. Experiments were not being documented. People
didn't clean up after themselves. Some of them did good work because they were self-motivated, but there was no accountability."

Even then, Debbie didn't take charge. "I felt like it wasn't my lab. These people were here before me, and I sort of missed my chance to impose order when I first arrived. The longer I accepted the situation, the less I felt justified in making big changes. But I finally got fed up with the situation and decided I had to start holding people accountable. I called a team meeting and told people that the situation was unacceptable and that I wasn't going to tolerate it anymore," Debbie said. "I told them I was going to make a lot of changes. I wasn't going to make up any new rules. I was just going to start insisting that the established rules be followed. People complained, 'But we've always done it this way. You've been here for four years and you've never enforced these rules.'

"I didn't blame them. I blamed myself," Debbie continued. "It was so liberating to take responsibility for that failure. It was all my fault. Not theirs. I just said, 'You are absolutely right! I have been lax. Not anymore!' I told them that I was sorry for being a weak manager and that I was going to be a much better manager moving forward. I went over the rules in detail, over all the standard operating procedures that we'd been ignoring. I explained that I was absolutely going to start enforcing those rules, and I explained how I was going to do that.

"I knew I was going to get plenty of resistance, especially from one employee, Gus, who had been working for the company for about twenty years." When Debbie began holding her team accountable, Gus, who had a positive paper trail from his years in the company, really pushed back, saying, "This is my company, too, and I've done things my way for some time and I've been successful." What did Debbie do? "I just kept communicating the old rules and my new policy. I was communicating the rules vividly and relentlessly." Gus thought that he would get

Debbie to back down. He figured his track record in the organization would protect him from any adverse consequences Debbie might try to impose. And he was right, at least for some time. Debbie's response? "I started creating the next chapter in Gus's track record." This approach is enough to get most employees to back down and make the necessary adjustments. But not Gus.

Some time later, I got an e-mail from Debbie. The subject line read, "A NEW DAY has dawned!" In the e-mail, she told me, "I knew a lot of the researchers didn't believe that I would follow through. But I stuck with it, and they finally got the message. These changes are not going away. The lab is already so much cleaner than it ever was before. We are actually following procedures for the first time since I've been here. Researchers are signing in and out the way they are supposed to and following safety procedures. We've gotten more work done in this lab in the last two weeks than we did in the entire year before." Even Gus? "I think Gus realized I wasn't going to back down ... so he started looking for another manager ... he moved upstairs to a new job today!"

Debbie concluded, "I just needed the guts to take charge. I only wish I had done this on day one."

Complication Number Four: "I'm a brand-new manager ... or brand new to the team."

You finally got that promotion you were hoping for. You are still working on the same team, but now you are in charge. All of a sudden, you find yourself managing people who were your peers yesterday, and today they are supposed to treat you like the boss. Managers often ask me, "How do I get them to respect my authority?"

I always tell new managers, "Remember, you are the one who got the promotion. Live up to it." As tempting as it might be to remain one of the guys, you are in a different role now. That doesn't mean you have license to act like a jerk. But you do have to take charge. Do not make the mistake of justifying why you got the promotion instead of someone else; do not explain why you should be the boss. Simply explain how you are going to behave as the boss. Explain what your expectations are and hold your employees accountable for meeting those expectations.

I got this piece of wisdom from a young carpenter who was made foreman of a crew he had worked on for several years. He told me, "You can't let the guys use that to put you on the defensive. They would tell me, 'Come on, Jim. You know how it is.' And I would always come back with 'Yeah. I do know how it is. I've been in your shoes, and I know that what I'm asking you to do is totally doable.'" Jim continued, "You've done the job that you are managing now, so use that to make yourself a better boss. I try to remember what it was like to do the job before I made foreman ... I think, 'What kind of things would have really helped me in this situation?' You have to use your experience to help the guys do a better job."

When you get that promotion and all of sudden you are the boss, you have two choices: behave in such a way that your former peers wonder why you are the new boss instead of one of them, or else behave in such a way that the answer to that question is so obvious that nobody would ever wonder. Let them know what kind of boss you will be. Let them know how you do business. Communicate the rules clearly: "This is the way to succeed working for me. This is how to earn what you need." Hold them accountable for their actions—tie their performance to rewards and detriments every step of the way.

Complication Number Five: "Some of the people I'm supposed to be managing are my friends."

Managers tell me every day about confrontations with employees who, when held accountable for their actions, turn around and protest, "But I thought we were friends!" This is what I tell them: Say to that employee, "Hey, next week, we are not going to pay you, but I was wondering if you'd be willing to come in and work really hard anyway to make me look good ... you know, since we are such good friends." What do you think that employee would say? "Hey, buddy, no hard feelings, but this is a job ... " And you should say, "Ding! No hard feelings, but I'm the boss."

Often, people become friends in the course of working together. Sometimes the friendship predates the working relationship. Either way, it can be hard to separate your role as boss from your role as friend. But you have to do it anyway.

First, decide which is more important to you. If the friendship is more important, maybe you shouldn't be the boss. Accept the fact that your role as boss might compromise or damage the friendship. Maybe you'll decide that you cannot risk your friendship and cannot work with that friend at all. Or maybe you'll decide that you cannot risk your friendship, and thus you don't want to be her boss. But someone has to be the boss. Wouldn't it be ironic if you turn down the job and your friend ends up being your boss instead of the other way around?

Second, protect the friendship by establishing ground rules that keep the roles separate. One restaurant manager told me about a good friend with lots of experience who wanted to work in her restaurant. She hired the friend, but made the ground rules very clear: "Our friendship is very important to me. My job is also very important to me, and around here I am the boss.

When we are here at work, I need to be the boss. When we are outside work, we try to leave that behind."

Third, protect the friendship by being a good boss. Make sure things go really well at work. Minimize the number of problems, and you will minimize the number of potential conflicts in your personal relationship.

Fourth, recognize and embrace the fact that the work you and your friend have in common will become more and more the terrain of your friendship. That's okay. With any luck, you both find the work you share to be interesting and important. If your friendship developed at work in the first place, the work you have in common was your original connection anyway. If your friendship predates the work relationship, then your friendship is going to change. At work, you can continue to maintain your rapport and build your friendship around the work. Outside of work, unless you make an ironclad rule that you won't discuss work, you will probably discuss work plenty.

As much as you try to keep work separate from your friendship and your friendship separate from your work, the boundaries will always be fuzzy. The best you can do is honor your friendship by being a great boss and hope that your friend will honor your friendship by letting you do that to the best of your ability.

Complication Number Six: "I don't have direct authority over certain employees, but I still have to manage them."

It you are deputized, say, as a short-term project leader, for the duration of that project, you simply must take charge. Ask your boss to sit down with the whole team and explain exactly what role each person is expected to play. If you are expected to be the leader, that must be made clear to every person on the team.

In other cases, managers have told me that they are dependent on other managers who are peers, not employees who report to them. Or else the manager might have to depend on other managers in parallel organizations (in a matrix structure). Or the manager has to manage partners in other businesses to complete a project (like a carpenter who has to work with the plumber and the electrician who are critical to the job but don't work for the carpenter). In some cases, the manager is struggling to manage a customer or client.

In all of these cases, you do not have direct authority. So what do you do? Your only option is to use influence to hold them accountable. What are the potential sources of your influence?

First, draw on your interpersonal influence; that is, the accumulated weight of your relationship with the person you are managing. Have you had personal rapport in the past? Will you have personal rapport in the future?

Second, influence people through the persuasiveness of good reasons. One manager in a large financial services firm told me that she has to depend every day on people who do not answer to her in any formal way. So she makes them answer to her strong logic: "I never ask for anything without making a convincing case for why it is necessary. I'm always selling: 'This is why you should do this for me. This is why it's a good thing for you, your team, and your company. This is why you should put my request first. This is why nothing else should get in the way.' I know I'm pushy, but the reason it works is that they are persuaded by my logic that they really should do what I'm asking them to do."

Third, draw on transactional influence. If you reach an agreement with a person, then you have reason to expect that agreement will be fulfilled. This is especially true of mutual recipro-cal promises. Even if you elicit a one-way promise from another person, if it has sufficient specificity, there is great pressure on the person to deliver on that promise. Have you relied on each other in the past? Will you rely on each other in the future?

Fourth, ask yourself, even if you don't have explicit author-ity in the relationship, are there consequences you can impose? Are there any rewards or detriments in your control?

Complication Number Seven: "I manage people do-ing work in areas in which I don't have knowledge or experience."

At first glance, this complication sounds peculiar. If you don't have any knowledge or experience and the employee knows the work much better than you do, then why are you that person's boss?

There are several common scenarios. Sometimes this hap-pens when companies separate technical tracks from manage-ment tracks. Those on the management track get further and further away from their technical background and get rusty on technical matters. In some cases, the manager might have one or more team members who play particular roles that are tan-gential to the rest of the team such as the "computer guy" or the bookkeeper. In other cases, the manager might be respon-sible for a cross-functional team in which each employee has a different area of expertise: for example, a software person, a hardware person, an engineer, a finance person, and a market-ing person. How can one manager have expertise in all of those areas? But probably the most common scenario is simply the case of the manager who delegates an area of responsibility to an employee, such as a customer account or an internal process or resource, and over time the employee becomes the in-house expert when it comes to that responsibility.

So how do you hold employees accountable when confronted with this complication? Learn. You don't have to become an expert on the work that person is doing. But you do have to learn enough to manage that person. How do you learn? Learn by managing that person closely over time. Sometimes you have to shadow the employee for a while. Watch him work. See what he actually does and how.

Think of yourself as a shrewd client and the employee as a professional you've hired. You don't have to be a doctor to make sure your doctor is doing a good job for you. It's okay that you don't know or understand everything the person is doing. But it's not okay to remain in the dark and trust. Be a smart, assertive, careful patient/client. Do your homework so that you can ask good probing questions every step of the way. If you don't understand the answers, say so. Ask more questions. Don't allow yourself to be brushed off. Get a second opinion—and a third. When you are spelling out expectations, focus on outcomes and ask lots of questions: "Exactly what are you going to do? Why? How are you going to do that? Why? What are the steps? What is involved in each step? How long will each step take? Why? What are the guidelines and specifications?" If the answers are vague, press for details. If the answers are complex, ask for explanations.

As you monitor and measure performance, stay focused on outcomes. Look at the work product and keep asking questions: "Did you do what you said you were going to do? Why or why not? How did you do it? How long did each step take? Why?" Again, press for details and ask for explanations. And don't forget to ask around. Ask customers, clients, vendors, coworkers, and other managers. Ask another employee who does similar work. Get those second and third opinions whenever you can. Document the basics of your conversations. What expectations were established? How did the performance line up with the expectations? As you are documenting performance, ask the expert employee to tell you what he thinks you should document and why.

Over time, of course, you will get to know the person's work better and better. You may never become an expert, but you will know more and more. You will get to know the employee's work habits and track record. You will be better able to gauge the employee's veracity, trustworthiness, and reliability. You will be able to tell if the person is on track or off track. You will be able to read the conversations you are having by the way the person talks and the kinds of things he says. Certainly, you will learn enough to be a good boss.

Make Accountability Real

You are the key to making accountability real. You are the keeper of the process.

- Make sure that your employees know that they will have to explain their actions to you up close and often.

- Tie every employee's actions to real consequences—rewards and punishments.

- Make sure that your employees know in advance that you will hold them accountable for their actions, so they can adjust their behavior accordingly before it's too late.

- Focus on actions the employee can control.

- Be the boss who is known for holding people accountable.

- Raise your standards.

- Take charge on day one … Today is always day one.

- Separate your role as the boss from your personal relationships.

- If you have no authority, use influence.

- If you don't have the expertise, act like a very shrewd client.

Sometimes all you have is the ability to ask people to explain or give an account of their actions. This type of interpersonal accountability in and of itself can be very powerful. That's one of the reasons it is so important to build relationships of trust and confidence with the people you manage. You need their trust and confidence most when they have to give answers to you. You want them to care about what you think of them. You want them to have a hard time looking you in the face and saying, after you've spelled out clearly what is expected of them, "No. I didn't do it."

CHAPTER 6

Tell People What to Do and How to Do It

You have a meaty new project for one of your very capable employees, Sam. Sam is inexperienced, but bright and eager—that's why you picked him for this project. You hand Sam a large stack of documents and tell him, "The first thing I want you to do is read through all this material and get a feel for what's going on here." Then you describe the genesis of the project, the other relevant players, and the overall goal. You tell Sam, "I'm not entirely sure what the final result should look like. What do you think?" This leads to a good discussion, but, in the end, you don't specify any concrete deliverable. You suggest that Sam get some input from his colleague, Barb, who did a similar project recently. You and Sam agree that he will "figure it out" as he goes along. After a half hour, you wrap up your talk with Sam by letting him know that this project is a priority. "What is the deadline?" Sam wants to know. You reply, "As soon as you can get it done." As Sam walks away with his armload of documents, you ask him to touch base with you in a few days to make sure things are going forward smoothly.

Chances are that you've just set Sam up for failure. For certain, you've guaranteed that Sam will accomplish less than he is capable of achieving on this project. He will have to spend days or weeks reinventing the wheel just to figure out what the project actually requires so that he can clearly define concrete deliverables for himself. And he might get it wrong. Even if he gets it right, he might not finish the project in time. After all, there probably *is* a real deadline, even though Sam won't learn about it until well into the project. If Sam is really good and really lucky, he might pull it off. Even then, Sam will almost surely have to make significant changes to the end product. It could easily turn out that there are important specifications that Sam never even knew about. And the changes will have to be made in a tremendous hurry. Sam will surely think, "Why didn't you tell me all this in the first place?"

Whatever the outcome of this project, Sam is likely to have a negative experience, and the resulting end product will be less than it could be. But how can you possibly hold Sam accountable for his work on this project? The manager is certainly at fault for failing to tell him what to do and how to do it in advance.

Without Clear Expectations, Accountability Means Nothing

Remember that the first and most important element in creating real accountability is spelling out expectations up front in clear terms. If you are the boss, your number one responsibility is to make absolutely sure that every person you manage understands exactly what he is expected to do and exactly how he is expected to do it.

It is amazing how many managers protest, "I shouldn't have to tell my employees what to do and how to do it. They should know how to do their jobs already." But then in the next breath, these same managers complain that some of their employees fail to meet expectations often and that most of their employees fail to meet expectations at least some of the time. How are employees supposed to meet—much less exceed—expectations if nobody tells them in clear, simple terms exactly what's expected of them?

And yet most managers hesitate to give orders. They don't want to boss people around. They argue: "One way conversations are no good. I prefer to ask employees lots of questions and seek their input. I listen and make suggestions and try to lead them to the right conclusions. But I allow employees to reach those conclusions on their own. Sometimes employees need to make their own mistakes and learn from them so that they can learn and grow. I want them to own their projects."

It is simply a fallacy that rehearsing wrong ways of doing things is a good way to learn how to do things right. If an employee reinvents the wheel every time, she will probably spend a lot of time practicing and learning bad techniques that will have to be unlearned. Trial and error is a good way of solving a new problem; it is not a good way of learning best practices. And it's certainly not a way to get employees to take ownership of their work. In fact, do employees ever really own their jobs ... or are they paid to do very specific tasks within closely defined parameters? Is what they do and how they do it ever really up to them? Employees only *own* their jobs—to the extent they possibly can—precisely when managers clarify exactly what they are supposed to do and how they are supposed to do it.

The truth is that most managers adopt this "facilitative" approach to managing—rather than an explicitly "directive" approach—because it's much easier to sidestep the uncomfortable tension that comes from telling other people exactly what to do.

But real managers give orders. Orders are simply mandatory directions. If you don't like the idea of giving orders, think of it as placing an order with a vendor. Imagine that your employee is a free agent, in business for herself, and you are the customer. Every time you give an assignment to your employee, imagine that you are placing a work order or a contract with a vendor: Are all the terms of the order spelled out? Have you clearly stated the service or product—including its specifications and delivery date—you will receive in exchange for payment? If you expect an employee to do anything at all, you need to tell him exactly what to do. If you expect him to do it one way as opposed to another, you must tell him exactly what specifications you expect him to follow.

If you truly believe in being a facilitative manager rather than a directive one, then you need to be a very aggressive facilitator. Yes, management conversations should be interactive dialogues. That means you need to ask really good questions.

- Ask basic questions: "Can you do this? Are you sure? What do you need from me?"

- Ask probing questions: "How are you going to do that? How are you going to start? What steps will you follow?"

- Ask short, focalizing questions: "How long will this step take? How long will that step take? What does your checklist look like?"

How hard should you try to let employees reach the right conclusions on their own? That depends on how much extra time you have. Be prepared for a lot of wild goose chasing in the conversation. Do you have time for that?

Ask an employee to think out loud about how she might approach an assignment but then skillfully lead the employee to the right conclusions as fast as possible.

- Listen to what the employee says carefully and quickly evaluate how well the employee understands the requirements of the task at hand.

- Pay close attention to the gaps in her approach.

- Keep asking the employee to think out loud until the approach she imagines is gap free.

Facilitate. Ask questions. Seek input. Let people think out loud. Make suggestions. But never forget that your job is to make sure that every single employee knows every step of the way exactly what is expected of her, what she is supposed to do, and how she is supposed to do it.

How Can You Maintain Clear Expectations When Expectations Change Every Day?

Quite a few managers are actually embarrassed that things change so frequently—as if change is somehow evidence that they don't really know what the heck they are doing. Managers cringe when they tell employees, "I know that yesterday I said the most important things were A, B, and C. Well, from now on they don't matter. Sorry about all that work we started doing on them. Now the most important things are X, Y, and Z ..."

Don't be embarrassed that things change. It wasn't your idea. Uncertainty is the new certainty, right? When priorities change, expectations change. That is just further evidence that telling people what to do and how to do it is critical. After all, who is going to tell each employee:

- Which priorities have shifted and changed today?

- What are they supposed to focus on today?

- What are the expectations today?

I'm afraid that's you again. After all, you are the boss.

If You Focus on It, It Will Get Done

If you've ever worked in the restaurant industry, you know that a restaurant is a high-pressure workplace. Everyone is in constant motion, everyone is in a hurry, everyone is multitasking, and everyone works with and depends on one another. How do restaurant managers keep things moving smoothly? An old sage of the industry once told me, "The manager has to make things happen, walking from the back of the house to the front of the house and then back again, barking orders the whole time. I go by the rule 'If you don't focus on it, it's not going to get done. If you focus on it, it will get done.'"

Another thing to know about the restaurant industry is that profit margins are slim. Because food can be one of the biggest variable costs in a restaurant, it's important to control food costs. Ultimately, that means controlling portion sizes and waste. One of my clients is a medium-sized restaurant chain that went through a steady period of growth, adding many new restaurants to the company in just a few years. During that growth period, the company lost control of food portions. New employees in the recently added restaurants were simply serving too much food. The problem was not a lack of portion guidelines. The problem was that the portion guidelines were not being followed. The COO of the company told me, "After a few months, we could see we had a big problem. I'm talking about millions of dollars potentially. It was a trend we couldn't afford. We absolutely had to get portions under control."

What did they do? "We made new portion guidelines that were easier to follow and distributed serving tools that corresponded to portion sizes. But the most effective thing we did is, every morning the district managers called and reminded the GM [general manager] of each restaurant to focus on controlling portions. So every day, each GM would talk to the chef and the kitchen staff to focus them on using the portion guidelines and new serving tools." Did it work? "Within days—I mean days—the food costs plummeted," the executive told me.

Focus on it and it will get done.

Develop an Obsession with Standard Operating Procedures

The food costs at the restaurant chain plummeted— except for the meat loaf and roast beef budgets. Those costs didn't budge. Why? "We realized that meat loaf and roast beef both have to be cut in the kitchen. The old guideline said that each portion should be a quarter-inch cut. The new guideline called for a quarter-inch cut as well, and even showed a picture of a quarter-inch cut. But the cooks were eyeballing it when cutting the meat—and they were eyeballing it a little thick. As a result, they were cutting into whole new pieces of meat unnecessarily, leading to a lot of waste."

What was the solution? "We talked to chefs in other restaurants who sold plenty of meat loaf and roast beef but consistently kept their meat loaf and roast beef costs under budget. It turned out there was a trick they all seemed to know: They used a quarter-inch spatula as a guide. It was that simple. We realized that we absolutely had to get this best practice out to the rest of the kitchens. We had to make this a standard operating procedure."

It's amazing how often best practices remain hidden below the radar in companies. Smart companies are always looking for experienced people on the front line who have developed the most effective way to accomplish a task or responsibility. When they identify a better way to do something, they call it a "best practice." But the real trick is getting employees throughout the company to adopt these best practices.

The best way to engage employees in adopting best practices is to convert them into standard operating procedures—and then require employees to follow those procedures precisely. Some companies are better at doing this than others.

A senior partner in an accounting firm put it this way, "If I were keeping someone's books, I would use a general ledger system. Right? I'm not going to wing it ... The same is true of conducting an audit. There are very specific steps you have to follow when conducting an audit. All of our professionals know that ... We've extended that logic to all the work done in this firm. We have checklists for everything. And we require people to use them."

An official in a nuclear weapons research facility put it this way: "We have an obsession with standard operating procedures around here. If we fail to use standard operating procedures, there could be a disaster of epic proportions. But that disaster is never going to happen because nobody here would ever think of deviating from procedures. We have step-by-step procedures for every single task in this facility and everybody uses them, which pretty much guarantees that everything will run without a hitch." The same rigor is standard in airplane cockpits and hospital operating rooms: Step-by-step checklists guide seasoned professionals through standard operating procedure every time.

Any time you have well-trained personnel doing critical work, you will see the rigorous use of standard operating procedures and checklists. That's because the rigorous use of standard operating procedures and checklists always reduces error rates, while improving quality and efficiency. By requiring employees to follow step-by-step checklists, you are telling each employee exactly what to do and how to do each task—you also make it a whole lot easier to hold them accountable.

"I'm Gonna Tattoo It on Your Forearm"

Let me give you another example from the restaurant industry. This is a story about batching French fries. One of my clients, a family-style restaurant chain with table service, serves fries—a choice of regular or spiced fries—with many of its meal choices. Typically, if you order fries in a restaurant and they arrive soggy and barely warm, the fry cook is probably "batching" fries; that is, making a large batch of fries so they are ready to serve as soon as they are ordered. A large batch of regular fries and a large batch of spiced fries prepared just before the lunch rush will often get the chef through half a busy lunchtime—a tempting shortcut to a cook trying to manage the chaos of a busy mealtime. Batching fries is certainly easier—and less chaotic—than frying a steady stream of fries throughout the meal.

The problem? Most people hate cold, soggy fries and will send them back when they get them. Waiters have to go back to the kitchen for more fries, but those won't be hot, either. Thus, customers get more cold, soggy fries, leave smaller tips, and potentially never come back to the restaurant. In short, it's not good to serve cold, soggy fries.

The solution, said one experienced manager, is simple: "Don't batch fries! If you are a fry cook, you can get into a rhythm, making fries as the orders are coming in. Yes, it's much harder on the fry cook, but you just have to make it clear, 'We don't batch fries!' A couple of years ago, I told one guy, 'I'm gonna tattoo it on your forearm: Don't batch fries!'"

Another manager put it this way: "You have to nag, nag, nag: 'Make half a basket, make half a basket, make half a basket.' I'm like a broken record. But if you come to my restaurant, you're going to get hot fries. I believe as a manager you have to 'follow up, follow up, follow up.' That's how you get results." I was not a bit surprised when I found out later that this restaurant manager had consistently achieved among the very best numbers in the company—year after year.

Lessons learned?

- Turn best practices into standard operating procedures.

- Teach standard operating procedures to everyone and require their use.

- Nag, nag, nag about standard operating procedures until you sound like a broken record.

- Give employees step-by-step checklists whenever possible.

- Follow up, follow up, follow up.

Every Assignment Has Parameters

Some jobs actually require employees to take risks and make mistakes, such as jobs that are by nature about being creative and innovative. The whole idea is to create something new and different. In that case, how is it possible to tell employees exactly what to do and how to do it?

If an employee's job is to be creative, the biggest favor you can do for that employee is to be clear about what is *not* within the employee's discretion. Spell out the parameters within which the employee ought to operate. If you don't want to hold the employee back in any way—no guidelines, no goals—clearly define whatever parameters *can* be established. Is there a time limit? Or will you pay the employee to brainstorm ad infinitum? How will you know when the employee is "done"? How will you recognize a finished product or result? If you want an employee to feel free to take risks and make mistakes, then what you need to do is spell that out as a concrete assignment: "I want you to take risks and make mistakes." Maybe you need to tell the employee how many risks to take and how many mistakes to make. Maybe not. But you have to define parameters in order to create a space in which risk taking and mistakes are truly safe in the context of a job.

Sometimes when managers give out "creative" assignments, what's really going on is that they don't have a clear goal in mind; they don't know what they are looking for ... yet. So they ask an employee to "take a crack at it," so they will have something to look at and can take it from there. This is nothing more than a manager using an employee to work out the early stages of his or her creative process. But if the manager has not explained to the employee what her role in the assignment is, it can turn into a frustrating experience. The employee works hard on a project, only to have her manager send it back to the drawing board over and over or take over entirely to rework it himself. The employee feels that the manager has hijacked the project and that her work and efforts have been for nothing.

Even if the goals of an assignment are uncertain, it is still critical that you tell an employee what you *do* know about the assignment and what role you want her to play in it. Tell her, "I don't know what I'm looking for yet, but I need you to take a crack at it so I have a starting point. Let me be clear. This is my project and I'm asking you to help jump-start the creative process. I am asking you to come up with a rough draft, which I will probably send back to the drawing board several times. It is likely that at some point I'll take over the project and rework it. This assignment needs to be completed by such and such date. Do you think you are up for it?"

Every assignment has parameters. As the boss, you must clearly and meticulously articulate those parameters—however few or loose they might be—so employees understand exactly what is expected of them.

Micromanagement versus Undermanagement

In chapter 1, I argued that micromanagement is largely a big red herring. Usually, what people refer to as micromanagement is, in fact, an example of undermanagement—managers not telling their employees what to do and how to do it. But, of course, there are cases in which managers overdo it.

For example, if a manager stands over the shoulder of a carpenter and tells him, "Nail number one goes right here." BANG, BANG, BANG. "Okay?" Then he says, "Nail number two goes there." BANG, BANG, BANG. But then he grabs the hammer and takes over: "Not there. Here." BANG, BANG, BANG. "Okay? Now I'm going to put nail number three right there." BANG, BANG, BANG. Maybe this is a real case of micromanagement: One hammer, two people. The manager is using the employee as a marionette to accomplish the task.

So, which is worse: micromanagement or undermanagement? If you had to choose between them, which one would you pick?

What goes wrong when you undermanage? Fires get started that never would have happened. Fires get out of control that could have been put out easily. Resources are squandered. People go in the wrong direction for days or weeks on end before anybody notices. Low performers hide out and collect a paycheck. Mediocre performers mistake themselves for high performers. High performers get frustrated and start looking for another job. And managers do lots of tasks that should be delegated to someone else. On top of all that, when you undermanage, you don't find out about these problems until after they cause a crisis.

Now let's see what happens when you overdo it and slip into real micromanagement—one hammer, two people. What goes wrong then?

You irritate your employees.

That's about it. The good news is that if you are managing too closely, you'll probably realize that pretty quickly. At that point, you just need to step back a little. No harm done. If I had to choose, I'd risk micromanaging.

By the way, take another look at that micromanagement story above featuring the carpenter. What if it is the carpenter's first day of work? What if the foreman is actually teaching the new carpenter best practices one small step at a time? In that case, it's not micromanagement at all. Right? It's support and development.

Delegation Is the True Art of Empowerment

If there is such a thing as micromanagement, then surely delegation is the antidote. Some managers make the mistake of thinking that delegation is about letting go. Sadly, delegation is not at all about letting go of work. Delegation is all about getting work done through others—and that is an intense, hands-on endeavor.

Delegation is the true art of empowerment, but it turns out to be a rather mundane art: it is simply clearly articulating goals, specifications, and deadlines. It might look something like this: "I want you to create a box by Tuesday at 3:00 p.m. It must be a wooden box, smaller than a refrigerator and bigger than a breadbox. It cannot be yellow, though gold is an option.

(Do you understand the difference between yellow and gold?) Those are the specifications. Everything else is up to you. Do you understand? Let's write that down, as if it were a work order."

The real trick to effective delegation is figuring out the goals, guidelines, and timelines that are appropriate for each employee with each assignment: How big should the goals be? How far out should the deadlines be? How many guidelines are necessary with each goal? These are always moving targets. That's why the manager should never think he can just bow out of the action. Even the best employees have bad days or face new challenges that require the manager's attention.

Here's a simple rule that will serve you well whenever delegating: Start small. If an employee delivers on a small goal with a short deadline and meets all the specifications, then delegate a project with a more ambitious goal or a constellation of goals and a longer deadline. As an employee demonstrates proficiency and performance, gradually increase the amount and importance of the work you assign, until you reach that person's appropriate scope of responsibility. Once that employee reaches that point, you can continue to empower him by using project planning tools together. Help him develop long-term project plans, complete with clear benchmarks along the way. Focus your one-on-one meetings on evaluating his progress toward each benchmark. Provide feedback and recommend adjustments every step of the way. Over time, he will be able to handle even bigger, more complex projects. The rigorous use of project planning tools is another well-kept secret ingredient of real empowerment.

Over time, effective delegation creates real empowerment because it clearly defines the terrain on which the employee has power, and all the while teaches employees how to manage themselves.

Here's the good news. When you tell employees what to do and how to do it over and over, they start doing what you want them to do the way you want them to do it. Hammer away at standard operating procedures and provide step-by-step checklists and people start following them. When they follow standard operating procedures, employees learn best practices through sheer repetition. Teach employees great habits by delegating effectively, demonstrating that self-management involves a constant accounting: What is expected of me? How is my performance measuring up to those expectations? What can I do to improve? What do I need to revise and adjust? Help each employee learn to constantly clarify priorities, expectations, plans, action steps, and timelines. Over time, through hands-on delegation, you can expand each employee's scope of responsibility.

CHAPTER 7

Track Performance Every Step of the Way

Think about a boss who keeps track of your day-to-day performance and that of every other employee on your team. She knows what you've worked on in the past, what you are working on now, and what you are going to be working on next. One of her mantras is "Let's write that down." She is constantly taking thorough, organized, and accurate notes, and then referring to them in subsequent conversations. In fact, you both use her written tracking system so much to guide your work that when it comes time for your annual review, there are never any surprises. This is a boss who is all over the details. She is a boss who is powerful, a boss who holds you accountable. She is a boss you respect. Right?

Now think about a boss who doesn't keep track of your day-to-day performance, or that of other employees on your team. She never seems to know who is doing what or why they are doing it. She often does not know the whereabouts of her employees; in fact, she seems to know nothing more than the basic information about the work of her employees. She is most definitely out of the loop; she cannot hold her employees accountable, and gets very little respect from them.

Which manager are you? Are you all over the details, or are you totally out of the loop? My guess is that you—like most managers—are somewhere in the middle.

When it comes to tracking employee performance, most managers keep a record of things like hours worked, self-presentation, and bottom-line numbers that appear in weekly or monthly reports. Otherwise, most managers monitor employee performance only incidentally, when they happen to observe the employee working; if they are presented with the employee's work product; if there is a big win; or if there is a notable problem. They rarely document employee performance unless they are required to do so, leaving no written track record other than those bottom-line reports that tell so little about the day-to-day actions of each employee.

The less knowledge you have about your employees' day-to-day work, the more out of touch you will be as a manager and the less power you'll have to:

- Provide guidance, direction, on-the-job training, and coaching.

- Identify resource needs.

- Anticipate problems and correct small routine errors as they occur.

- Keep employee conflicts to a minimum.

- Prevent employees from behaving inappropriately.

- Keep everybody focused on the work.

- Set ambitious, but meaningful, goals and deadlines.

- Assess the appropriate scope of responsibility to delegate to employees.

- Evaluate performance against expectations.

- Hold your employees accountable for their actions.

- Motivate employees by fairly linking their performance to rewards or detriments.

- Prevent low and mediocre performers from becoming comfortable in their jobs.

- Prevent high performers from leaving.

- Help the best people develop into new leaders.

Knowledge Is Power

When you are the manager who is "all over the details," on the other hand, you will be respected and powerful due, if nothing else, to the very fact that you track performance so closely. Armed with knowledge about every employee and his work, you will be in a position to make judgments that will increase productivity, quality, and the work experience of your employees. You'll be in a position to set employees up for success every day and help them continually improve their work and develop their skills. If you have to impose some negative consequence, you'll be able to demonstrate that your decision is based on a detailed written record. When it comes time to reward high performers, you will have a detailed written record to help you make your case and secure more generous rewards.

Reputation means credibility. The greater your reputation for being all over the details, the more power you have—even if you are not knowledgeable in a particular situation. Why? People are much more likely to share information with you and answer your questions fully and honestly. After all, they will think, you might already have the information or answers to the questions you are asking. They also will be more attentive to the details of their work if they have confidence that you will be reviewing the details of their work. "Surveillance creates a lot of self-surveillance," I was once told by a leader in the intelligence community. "If people know someone is watching them, they tend to watch what they say and do a whole lot more carefully."

A manager at a research company told me the following: "I spot-check everybody's work. I go out of my way to notice small details. About once every week or two, with every person, I will point out some small detail in their work. Like 'You know that e-mail you sent to so-and-so at 10:13 a.m. last Friday? There was a mistake in the third sentence. Here, I printed out a copy so I could show you.' I'll tell you what. After I started doing that, everybody started being a lot more careful about details."

If you want to be the manager who is all over the details, you need a tracking system to document performance on a daily basis. Tracking performance in writing adds so much clarity to the management relationship. Simply talking about expectations and performance is not enough. Writing down the details allows you to confirm every step of the way with each employee: "Are you sure you understand? This is what I'm writing down. Take a look. Is this your understanding, too?"

Tracking in writing is also very powerful when it comes to creating psychological commitment to expectations that are agreed upon together. When you say something and then write it down in a running log, you are "memorializing" what was said in the form of a tangible piece of evidence. Even when there is no legal significance to a written document, there is an important impact. Both parties are sharing the experience of creating a written record that can be referred to again later and will trump any one person's memory. Sharing that experience and knowing that every expectation is included in a written record creates a lot of pressure to live up to the commitments made.

Sometimes you and your employee may have differing recollections about what was said, about what, and when. By tracking in writing, you have a record that resolves those disparate recollections. Beyond that, your records will help you justify giving individuals special rewards or detriments because you can point to performance as the reason and your documentation as proof of performance. That's even more important in the event of formal disputes. Whether you are facing a charge of unfair treatment or any type of complaint, those in HR and Legal are going to want to know "what's in the file." You should be able to tell them that you have a detailed contemporaneous record of all of your regular conversations with every employee. That documentation will provide you with a paper trail to support your version of the facts.

Tracking is also the key to ongoing performance improvement. Constant evaluation and feedback help you revise and adjust your marching orders: "You did a great job on A, B, and C. You did every item on the to-do list. You followed all the instructions. You followed all the rules. Great job. Now let's talk about D. On D, you failed to complete items 3, 4, and 5 on the to-do list. Why? What happened? Let's talk about how you are going to do items 3, 4, and 5. And now let's talk about E. On E, you missed the following details. Let's go over the checklist and talk about how you are going to fill in those details." Ultimately, this process of revising and adjusting performance is the key to growth and development, too.

In the real world, growth and development follow when a person's concrete actions are subjected to rigorous and honest evaluation on an ongoing basis and the person is able to use that information to practice and fine-tune. In order to do that, you have to keep score—in writing.

I was training a group of sales managers who, one time, furiously objected to the idea of regularly tracking performance in writing. So I asked them to describe the system their salespeople use for tracking their contacts with sales leads. It turns out they require salespeople to keep detailed records, including precise notes, dates, and times of conversations, of all their interactions with their customers and potential customers. Why did they insist that their salespeople keep such detailed tracking records? "Because these conversations really matter," they answered. "If you don't track your customer calls, your follow-up calls would be terrible. You wouldn't be able to make any sales. The ability to make reference back to specific things that were said in previous conversations helps you maintain control of the conversation."

In other words, they need their salespeople to be all over the details. The same is true of the core tasks of any competent professional. Imagine a doctor or nurse administering medicine to a patient in the hospital without making a notation in the patient's chart, a banker cashing a check without charging it against the right account in the bank system, or an insurance adjuster who pays claims but doesn't record them. All of these suggestions seem absurd. Yet managers interact with employees all the time without ever thinking to document those interactions.

Just as salespeople need to constantly refer back to their notes to ensure the success of their sales calls—as any professional must refer to ongoing records of ongoing activity to ensure continued success—you need to be able to reference your ongoing record of employee performance. Exactly what expectations, goals, deadlines, requirements were spelled out? What was discussed? You need to be able to point to written documentation.

Track Performance by Monitoring Concrete Actions

Unfortunately, the typical manager monitors mostly just the elements of performance that are easy to notice. Managers focus disproportionately on things like hours in the office because they can easily see when an employee arrives and leaves. Face time and personality have such undue weight simply because they are literally staring the manager right in the face. And then there are those online daily reports and weekly spreadsheets that are delivered right to a manager's computer screen or in-box. But all this business data or knowing exactly when an employee comes and goes doesn't tell you what an employee is actually doing in his office or workstation during those hours at work. Tracking concrete actions takes a lot more effort.

"When you start watching your employees more carefully and asking them a lot of questions about their work, you find out a lot of things you didn't know about what they are doing and how they are doing it. You find out things you really should have known in the first place," said one manager I'll call Jed.

Jed was managing an enthusiastic new employee, Kary, in the e-newsletter division of a research company. At first, Jed worked with Kary to teach her the process for sending out the e-newsletters. She quickly got the hang of the process, which was similar to the process she had used at the newspaper where she had worked previously. The problem, however, began when Kary had to learn a process with which she had no prior experience. Usually, whenever e-newsletters are sent out, some percentage of them bounce back because there is some problem with the transmission. Jed explained to Kary that it was critical that she go through each of the several hundred bounce backs she would get each time she sent out a batch of e-newsletters and resolve the problems quickly. "This is the kind of thing that has to be done every time you send the e-newsletter, or else your database quickly degrades and the percentage of bounce backs goes up and up and then you are failing to effectively distribute the newsletter," Jed told me.

"I went through the process with her, and she seemed to understand it. I even asked her about it every week at staff meetings. But I made a fatal error with Kary: I never actually checked her work. I didn't look closely at the database to see if she was making changes to the records each time the e-newsletter went out. She did every other part of the job so well. She had a great personality and a great attitude. She had no problem at all with sending the e-newsletters or adding or deleting subscribers when they actually e-mailed with a request. But she never really understood the bounce-back process."

This went on for four months before Jed became concerned because Kary was working way too many hours. "She was working twelve hours a day, and she was looking exhausted. Her energy and morale dropped quite a bit. She looked terrible and wasn't talking in staff meetings ... apparently, several of her coworkers knew exactly what was going on and had been urging her to talk to me about it. If I had asked around a little, I would have realized what was going on much sooner. When I finally had the sense to talk to her, it turned out that she was incredibly far behind on the bounce-back process. She was drowning in the backlog and still didn't really have a handle on the process.... Finally, I created detailed checklists for her with all the steps for trying to correct each record. Then I took a few tasks off her plate and gave her a couple of weeks to just work on the bounce-backs. She kept track of how many she was doing each day and she worked her way through that whole ocean of backlog. At the end of that process, she was a total pro at dealing with bounce-backs.... Ever since then, she gives me a report after every newsletter of exactly how many bounce-backs there were and how she dealt with them."

Jed concluded the story with this: "I really learned my lesson with Kary. You just can't take anything for granted. I should have been checking her work more closely. At least I should have asked around a little sooner."

There are five ways to monitor the concrete actions of employees.

Watch employees work. One of the most effective ways to monitor an employee's performance is with your own eyes. Watching an employee interact with a customer for a few minutes will tell you more about that employee's customer service performance than a batch of customer feedback surveys. That's why so many route-sales organizations encourage their managers to do ride-alongs with salespeople. So the manager can actually watch the employee do his job. If you are having difficulties helping an employee succeed with a particular task, "shadow" that employee while he does the task. You'll find out exactly what he's doing and how he can do it better.

Ask for an account. In every one-on-one conversation with every employee, ask for an account of what that person has done since your last conversation: "What concrete actions did you take? Did you meet the clearly spelled-out expectations?" Then listen very carefully, make judgments, and ask more probing questions. Asking for an account is the number one method for holding a person accountable for his actions. Then move on to discuss next steps. As long as you are consistently carrying out your one-on-one management conversations with every person on a regular basis, this element of monitoring performance will become routine.

Help employees use self-monitoring tools. You can also ask employees to help you keep track of their actions by using self-monitoring tools like project plans, checklists, and activity logs. Employees can monitor whether they are meeting goals and deadlines laid out in a project plan, make notations within checklists, and report to the manager at regular intervals. Activity logs are diaries that employees can keep, noting contemporaneously exactly what they do all day, including breaks and interruptions. Each time the employee moves on to a new activity, he is asked to note the time and the new activity he is turning to.

Review work in progress on a regular basis. Check your employees' work carefully in process along the way. If an employee is not responsible for producing a tangible end product, then watching that employee work is the same thing as reviewing work in progress. If she is responsible for an end product, spot-check it while she is working on it. For example, if the employee manages a database, spot-check the records. If the employee writes reports, look at drafts. If the employee makes phone calls, record them and listen to a random sample. If the employee makes widgets, check some half-done widgets and see how they look. You can't actually keep track of everything every employee does, but you can check random samples on a regular basis.

Ask around a little. Gather intelligence. Ask customers, vendors, coworkers, and other managers about their interactions with specific employees. Always ask questions about the employee's work, never about the person. Don't ask for evaluations, but ask for descriptions. Don't ask for impressions, but ask for details. And don't believe everything you hear; the unverified statements of third parties are simply hearsay. But the more you keep your ear to the ground, the more you know which sources can be trusted. So ask around on a regular basis.

What Gets Measured and What *Should* Get Measured?

Why do so many managers and employees often find the review process to be inadequate, incomplete, unfair, or downright capricious? Because reviews usually fail to accurately measure the employee's actual performance over the course of the previous four, six, or twelve months. Throughout the course of the year, managers rarely conduct an ongoing, explicit evaluation of each employee's concrete actions against clearly stated expectations. When prompted by HR to write reviews or rank their employees, they scramble to complete obtuse "measurements" because they are required to do so. How often do we hear about managers asking their employees to do a "first draft" of the review to give the manager something to work from, and fast, because the deadline is approaching? Usually, managers assemble evaluations, reviews, and rankings based on the scant records they have kept during the year.

In order to accurately evaluate an employee's performance, managers need to look at the concrete actions each employee takes every day to get his job done and then measure it against the expectations that were set in advance. On an ongoing basis, managers need to ask the following three questions:

1. Did the employee meet every goal that was set? Did he do all the tasks that he was required to do?

2. Did he complete his tasks according to the guidelines and specifications provided? Did he follow standard operating procedures?

3. Did he meet the deadlines set in advance?

If you have been monitoring, measuring, and documenting the concrete actions of your employees on a regular basis, answering these questions should simply require a cumulative summary of your regular tracking. This is the most important data you will ever have about an employee's true performance. Of course, you also have at your disposal an incredible amount of data in the form of daily, weekly, quarterly, or annual reports detailing all sorts of performance information—from attendance to hours worked, customer complaints, sales data, and on and on. Yes, you should use this information too—along with your own written performance tracking. But when using reports, study those numbers inside out and make sure you know exactly how those numbers are really tied to the real, concrete actions within the control of each individual employee. What are those numbers really telling you about each individual employee's actual performance?

For example, at first glance, sales numbers seem to be a clear and simple way of monitoring sales performance. But sometimes that's not the case. Let me show you. Salesperson #1 is selling a product that has no market reputation, and, on top of that, she is working from a list of unqualified customers who are not likely buyers of the product. Meanwhile, salesperson #2 is selling a product with a great market reputation, and he is working from a qualified list of likely buyers. It's quite likely that the numbers for salesperson #2 will be significantly better than those of salesperson #1—but for reasons that are actually beyond the control of the salespeople. In this case, the sales numbers do not offer enough information to adequately measure the performance of these two employees.

In fact, measuring the actual performance of each salesperson in the example above requires digging much deeper than looking at the numbers alone. How could you measure their performance? You could first look at the number of calls each salesperson attempted every day. At least that is an action that is within each salesperson's control. But even that won't tell you much about the quality of the salesperson's work. To accurately measure each salesperson's work, you should evaluate *how* each person handled each call. Is the salesperson listening carefully and not interrupting? Is she sticking to the script? Is she re-

sponding well to questions? Is she moving the conversation to a
close? Those kinds of questions are often the ones that matter
most when measuring performance. Sometimes the only fair
and accurate way to evaluate an employee's performance is to
exercise your own judgment as a manager.

Document Performance

Most managers rarely document performance unless they are
required to. Still, in the regular course of business, managers
often inadvertently create a paper trail of notes, paperwork,
end-product reviews, and, especially, e-mail correspondence.
Indeed, e-mail dialogues may be the only way in which a lot
of managers document the details of an employee's day-to-day
performance. Whether they realize it or not, when they use
e-mail, these managers are creating detailed written contemporaneous records to spell out expectations, evaluate work in
progress, praise employees, or lambaste them. But the bulk of
an employee's formal "file" is made up of quarterly or annual
reviews, development plans, rankings, numbers, perhaps occasional nominations for bonuses and awards, and, of course, any
formal write-ups of misconduct or persistent failure.

Often managers rigorously document performance when
one of their employees has serious performance problems. One
senior human resources executive explains, "Usually, a manager
calls when she wants to take some kind of disciplinary action
against an employee. So the HR specialist will ask the manager,
'How long has this been going on?' Usually, it's a problem that's
been going on for a long time. 'Have you been documenting
this problem?' The answer is, typically, 'No, not really.' The

problem has been going on for three years and the manager hasn't been documenting it at all, so HR can't do much to help this manager. Instead, we will provide the manager with a formal documentation process that will allow the manager to meet our requirements for taking disciplinary action. The process includes a date and time log for recording verbal requests and verbal warnings, as well as a process for written warnings. After the second written warning, the manager can put the employee on what we call a PIP."

PIP stands for performance improvement plan. PIPs are very common in the world of human resources. The PIP is considered a punitive disciplinary process that usually follows a number of verbal and written warnings. Here's how it works. The manager and the employee together set clear expectations and work out a plan for what the employee needs to do to improve performance. Goals are broken down into concrete steps and to-do lists with tight deadlines and guidelines and parameters are clearly spelled out. Every week, or sometimes every day, the manager is supposed to monitor the employee's performance very closely according to the plan and document regularly whether the employee's performance meets expectations.

In short, the standard punitive disciplinary process for employees with the most serious performance issues actually forces managers to do what *they should have been doing every step of the way anyway*! It should be no surprise that the PIP process succeeds about half the time in improving performance. The standard PIP actually covers the basics of managing. Amazing! If it works this well with employees who have developed track records of serious performance problems, imagine how well it works with employees who are already doing just fine.

Put every employee on a PIP. Call it something else if you

must. It shouldn't be used as a warning, a punishment, or a path out the door. It should become standard operating procedure for everyone. The standard performance improvement plan is the perfect format for documentation: The manager writes down expectations for the employee at the beginning of each week, then monitors and documents closely how the employee's concrete actions are meeting those expectations. That's exactly what every manager should be doing with every employee— good, bad, and average. Document how every employee's actions are meeting expectations every step of the way.

Create a Simple Process You Can Stick With

What you need is a process that is simple and easy to use, not a bunch of cumbersome paperwork to hold you back. You need a process that is practical so that you will stick to it.

Some managers keep a notebook or a diary in which they take management notes each day. Each time you make an entry, write down the employee's name and the time, and then make a note tracking that person's performance. Over time, you may find it useful to create a template for each employee that corresponds to his particular tasks and responsibilities to make note-taking that much easier.

Other managers use a simple relationship management software package to create an electronic manager's notebook. All you need is a database and scheduling program that allows you to create a data record for each employee you manage. In each record, there should be a space to take notes. This way, whenever you take notes, they are captured digitally and are automatically dated and time-stamped. Some managers go out of their way to cut and paste key e-mail correspondence with employees and keep them right in the notes section of that employee's record in the electronic manager's notebook. You can also customize the notes section in most relationship management packages, so you can insert special notes templates for each employee.

Whether you use a notebook or a software program, you need to capture certain key pieces of information.

Expectations. Goals and requirements that were spelled out. Instructions given or to-do lists assigned. Standard operating procedures, rules, or guidelines reviewed. Deadlines set.

Concrete actions. Write down observable facts only. What have you observed the employee doing while watching? What does the employee say when asked about his actual performance? What do his self-monitoring tools reveal? What does your ongoing review of work product tell you? What do you learn about the employee's actions when you ask around?

Measurements. How are the actions matching up against the expectations? Has the employee met requirements? Did he follow instructions, standard operating procedures, and rules? Did he meet his goals on time?

Be Careful What You Write Down

When you are writing things down, remember that you are creating a contemporaneous record that could become key documents in resolving disputes with an employee. Never describe an employee in any way; rather, describe the employee's performance. Don't write that an employee's performance is slow, incomplete, or inadequate. Write that the employee did not meet the stated goals by the stated deadlines. Write that the employee missed items A, B, and E on the to-do list. Write that the employee missed details on item C. Never call people names—ugly, stupid, lazy, and so on—and never even name behavior. Instead of naming, describe. Describe, describe, describe.

When Should You Document Performance?

Document performance every step of the way.

Before you sit down with an employee for a one-on-one meeting, check your notes from the last session. What performance did we go over together? What expectations were spelled out? And then ask yourself, why do I need to talk to this person today? What do I need to talk to this person about today? How? When? Where? Make some notes to yourself in preparation for your meeting. Outline the ground you want to cover: What actions do you want to ask the employee about? And what are the next steps you want to establish? What expectations do you want to set going forward? During the actual one-one-one meeting with the employee, ask the employee to give you an account of his actions, then spell out expectations and next steps. Make notes during the conversation as necessary. Make notes immediately after the conversation. In between one-on-one meetings, make sure to write down everything of consequence related to that employee's performance. If you think of something you want to mention in your next meeting with the person, write that down.

It's not always possible, practical, or necessary to show your written records to your employee. But if you can, showing your employee exactly what you are writing down creates clarity about expectations, reinforces the details and guidelines of the assignment, and increases the chances that the employee will commit to meeting her goals. Showing the employee your notes as you take them will also create an opportunity to correct any misunderstandings up front. Some of the best managers I know ask their employees to create their own parallel notebooks. As the manager writes things down, she can say, "I'm writing this down. What are you writing down? Are we on the same page?"

If You Are Really Tracking Performance That Closely, the Employee Can Hardly Fail

A human resources executive recently told me, "When a manager does his part in documenting performance, it allows HR to do our job. You should see what happens when we get a call from a manager who has actually been documenting performance. Bells and whistles go off. We yell out, 'Hey, we got one! We got a manager who is documenting performance!' That's how rare it is. If every manager had every employee on a PIP all the time, our job would be so easy," says the HR executive. "But then if every manager had every employee on a PIP all the time, it would make the manager's job much easier, too, in the end. If you are really tracking performance that closely, the employee can hardly fail." And if he does, "you get him right back on track immediately. You can really do that if you are tracking performance that closely."

CHAPTER 8

Solve Small Problems before They Turn into Big Problems

You hate confrontations with employees. They only seem to make things worse. Sometimes you even end up firing an employee. For these reasons, you generally avoid giving employees negative feedback unless it's absolutely necessary. When it comes to small performance issues, you don't come down like a ton of bricks; instead, you hint at a problem, making suggestions that will indirectly improve the situation—you hope. Sometimes if the problem seems relatively insignificant, you just let it slide. Yes, some employees take advantage of this, but you still hesitate to push too hard because you don't want to make a scene.

Those Dreaded Confrontations

The typical hands-off manager basically avoids performance problems until they can no longer be ignored. But problems always come up. And by the time a problem can no longer be avoided, the dreaded confrontation is inevitable.

Without regular daily or weekly management conversations with a strong focus, the manager has no natural venue in which to provide the employee with regular evaluation and feedback—good, bad, or neutral. Instead of regular and consistent "problem solving," which is a good thing, dealing with problems becomes a difficult conversation to be avoided. If small problems are dealt with at all, they are dealt with lightly and in passing, which means these problems are likely to recur. When the problem recurs, it might not be noticed, it might be let to slide, or it might be dealt with again, maybe lightly and in passing. That means the problem is likely to recur again. Sometimes small problems that recur incessantly cause managers to finally explode in an outburst of frustration or anger. Other times small problems recur incessantly and become part of the fabric of the workplace. But some small problems fester and grow. Over time, they become large problems.

By the time most "performance improvement" conversations actually take place, it's usually too late for the manager to be very effective. For one thing, solving a problem after it has already festered and grown large is so much more difficult than preventing that problem in the first place, or solving it while it was smaller. Now much time and energy has to be spent cleaning up the mess and restoring the status quo. For another thing, in the midst of a problem, people are never going to be at their best. The situation is urgent and people are stressed, frustrated, and in a hurry. Indeed, there are plenty of managers who don't really deal with problems until they get angry. And, of course, sometimes these conversations become heated.

On top of all that, employees often feel attacked when they

are confronted with a negative assessment of their behavior. These conversations often come as a shock, as if without warning, especially when the performance in question is a problem that has been festering for some time. The employee is likely to say or at least think, "I've been doing this same thing for days, weeks, or months, so why now all of a sudden are you coming down on me? Why didn't you talk to me about this problem sooner, before I built a track record of failure?" Often the manager starts to second-guess himself: "Do I have all the facts? Did I spell out expectations clearly? Am I being fair?" And the answers are probably no, no, and no. Plus, neither the manager nor the employee is experienced at having conversations with each other about the employee's performance, so neither the employee nor the manager is very good at it. Of course, these conversations are going to be difficult. Most performance improvement conversations are doomed before they even start.

These conversations are often followed by hours of fixing, salvaging, and cleaning up to get things back on track. This is often what managers mean when they say they spend all their management time "fighting fires, solving problems" and thus get behind on their "real" work. After solving a performance problem that never had to become so urgent in the first place, the typical manager convinces himself that he definitely doesn't have any more time to do any more managing. The manager goes right back to his hands-off undermanaging ways, awaiting the next unnecessary crisis, when he will spring into action once again.

Meanwhile, the employee is likely to feel demoralized. There are bad feelings. Sometimes it can be hard to bounce back and start feeling good about the job and the manager again. Often things get back to normal. But sometimes, especially after a very difficult confrontation between a manager and an employee, the situation goes downhill. The employee might even go into a downward spiral.

Do you want to be great at solving employee performance problems? Do you want to find it downright easy to tell employees when and how they need to improve? If you do, you need to anticipate and avoid one problem after another—and solve small problems whenever they crop up. If you engage in regular problem solving, nine out of ten performance problems will be solved quickly and easily or will be avoided altogether. In most cases, even long-standing problems will die away under the withering medicine of regular and consistent strong management.

Solve One Small Performance Problem at a Time

No problem is so small that it should be left alone; small problems too often fester and grow into bigger problems. Sometimes managers are afraid to nitpick. "After all," these managers say, "everybody makes mistakes. If a small problem occurs that is not likely to recur, doesn't it do more harm than good sometimes to focus on it?" It only does more harm than good if you focus on small problems to the exclusion of other important details (including small successes).

If you are talking with employees about the details of their work on a regular basis, then talking about small problems— whatever they may be— should be something you do as a matter of course. Solving small problems should be part of your ongoing dialogue with that employee. In this context, nitpicking is a good thing. It sends a message that high performance is the only option, that details matter, and that you are paying close attention. You are also doing the employee a favor by making her aware of the small problem so that she can fix it or avoid it in the future. Over time, you are doing the employee the added favor of helping her become more detail oriented.

This is not about perfectionism. Perfectionism is the disabling fear of completing a task, dressed up in the pursuit of an illusory quality standard. Zeroing in on small problems is about constant improvement. In the course of regular guidance and direction, addressing one small problem after another is what ongoing continuous performance improvement actually looks like. Constant evaluation and feedback help you revise and adjust your marching orders. In turn, the employee revises and adjusts her performance. Through this slow, steady progress, you help employees revise and adjust so they can keep practicing and fine-tuning. "Revise and adjust. Practice and fine-tune." That is the mantra of continuous improvement.

When you diagnose a performance problem, start focusing intensely in your regular management conversations on spelling out concrete solutions.

If an employee is often tardy, don't tell him to stop coming in late. Tell him to start coming in on time. Talk to him before he has a chance to be tardy again. At the end of his shift today, remind him exactly at what time he is supposed to arrive tomorrow. Ask him if he is giving himself enough time to get to work in the morning.

If an employee is failing to meet quality standards, don't tell her to stop missing details and ignoring specifications. Give her a checklist of every detail and specification she needs to get right. Talk it through in advance. Ask her to carry the checklist and check off each detail and specification as she completes them.

Don't ask an employee to stop swearing. Instead, teach him

to start saying alternative words, like "Dagnabbit!" "Gee whiz!" "Gosh!"

If an employee is too slow, set a realistic quota of tasks per hour or set realistic short-term deadlines with a clear timetable of benchmarks from beginning to the end. Suggest that she give herself a time limit to complete each task and stick to it.

If an employee is chatting too much at work, coach the employee on how to keep quiet and focus on the work all day.

Many of the most vexing employee performance problems seem intangible and therefore difficult to coach employees out of. How do you tell an employee how to have a better attitude, for example? If you want to see a bad attitude get much worse, try telling someone with a bad attitude that she has a bad attitude. Don't. It is never helpful to "name" a behavior if you are trying to get someone to change it. Instead, describe behavior.

Instead of saying, "You are in a bad mood this morning and that's really disruptive," try saying something like "At 9:13 a.m., you walked through the door. Instead of closing it gently, you pushed the doorknob swiftly and rather hard so that the door slammed shut, making a loud noise. Then you said in a very loud voice, 'This place sucks!' After that, you walked quickly to your desk, in such a way that every step you took made a loud thud." Finally, connect the behavior with concrete work outcomes: "This distracts other employees from their work. It makes other employees, including me, reluctant to talk to you even when they need things from you."

Then spell out the behavior you want to see instead: "Tomorrow, please come in by 9:00 a.m. When you open the door, please don't slam it shut; hold the handle and push the door gently. Try to smile and speak in a quiet voice. Walk slowly, so your steps are quiet. If you feel the urge to say something negative, bite your tongue. That's how I want you to arrive at work tomorrow and every day. Let's make that a standard operating procedure."

What if an employee lacks passion or enthusiasm for her work? Involve her more deeply in the project and teach her new skills. It is worth remembering that few people start out passionate or enthusiastic about anything. Most people need to do the job for a while before they feel any enthusiasm for it. Also, it's usually not what they are doing that makes them feel passionate, but rather *how* they are doing it. When people do something with purpose and precision, it is possible to unlock the joy in that work. It also helps when they do it with other people who care a lot about that work as well.

What if an employee is not disposed to take initiative? Provide that employee with an explicit list of "extra to-do items" to avoid downtime. Employees who lack initiative are often not sure what to do after they've completed their basic tasks. By providing them with extra to-do items, you are eliminating this uncertainty. Explain that when their normal work is done, they should move on to these extra items.

If an employee fails to take on enough responsibility, make tough decisions, or solve problems when they arise, work with that person very closely to develop decision/action tools. Talk through every circumstance you can foresee. For each one, provide very simple and clear marching orders to the employee: "If A happens, do X. If B happens, do Y. If C happens, do Z," and so on.

If an employee does his job just fine, but never goes the extra mile, describe the big picture for that person. Explain to the employee exactly what going the extra mile looks like and make sure the employee knows what's in it for her: "If you go the extra mile today by doing A, B, and C, then here's what I can do for you in return."

You'll be amazed at how many seemingly intangible issues can be made tangible just by doing the hard work of clarifying expectations. With some persistent coaching, you can help someone make a lasting and meaningful change on something as intangible as a bad attitude, lacking enthusiasm, or going the extra mile.

Conflict between Employees

One of the most difficult performance issues with which managers commonly struggle is conflicts between and among team members. These conflicts emerge from different sources. Sometimes people just don't like each other. Other times there are real gripes, personal and professional.

You cannot referee every argument. But you can make these conflicts a whole lot less likely to emerge by being the kind of boss who keeps every employee focused on getting work done. If you keep your employees busy with work, they have less time to have conflicts with each other. When you are coaching employees every day, spelling out expectations, and tracking performance every step of the way, employees are less likely to worry about each other and more likely to worry about getting their own work done. And the more focused everyone is on the work they have in common, the more likely they are to cooperate. When conflicts do happen, if you are all over the details, you will know what's in character and out of character for each person, what rings true and what doesn't. You will be in a better position to evaluate and make appropriate decisions.

If certain employees often clash with each other, then do what you can to keep them apart, working in different areas or on different shifts. If some employees are prone to conflicts, discuss this issue in your regular coaching dialogue with those individuals. Before there is another conflict, remind them how to avoid conflict and interact in positive ways with others. Tell them what to say and how to say it so that they can engage in conflict-free interactions.

If you have an unusual number of conflicts among your employees, it's critical that you figure out why that is. Most likely, you are part of the problem. If you are not spelling out expectations and tracking performance, employees blame each other for problems that occur and resent each other because there is no real accountability. The stronger the hand you take, the more likely you will be to squeeze out the airspace for a lot of these conflicts. But maybe it's not you. It could be that there is something about the way your team functions that is causing the conflicts. Is there a high level of interdependence, where team members have to rely on each other inordinately? Are there standard operating procedures in place to ensure that this interdependence flows smoothly? Maybe you can eliminate or improve aspects of your business process to reduce unnecessary conflict.

When Problems Persist

Some problems resist solutions even when you deal with them aggressively and persistently. Take a step back and ask yourself if you are missing something. Have you properly diagnosed the problem? Do you need to look at the problem in a new way? At this stage of the game, nearly all performance problems fall into one or more of three categories: ability, skill, or will.

- If the problem is ability, your employee's natural strengths are probably not a good match with some or all of the tasks and responsibilities in her current role. If this is the case, your best option is to change the tasks and responsibilities that are a poor match and replace them with work that is a better fit. If you cannot do that, you may have to face the fact that you have the wrong person for the job.

- If the problem is skill—an employee is missing knowledge, hasn't mastered techniques, or lacks necessary tools or resources—it is your job to make sure that the employee gets what she needs to succeed. Find the gaps in her skills and fill them by offering her training or the right tools and resources. If you cannot get her what she needs, it is your responsibility to work with that employee to figure out how to limp along as well as possible without it.

- The hardest nut to crack, of course, is motivation—the will to perform. Every person is different, so what motivates each person is different. But in the case of persistent performance problems, the real question is: "What demotivates a person?"

  Sometimes an employee has an internal issue, maybe a personality trait that is not going to go away. Maybe the employee has an actual physical or psychological pathology that requires the help of a trained therapist or doctor. If you have an employee who is underperforming due to an internal issue, your only option is to refer the employee to employee services or HR so that he can get professional help. You are not a doctor or a psychologist or a best friend. At work, you have to be the boss. Sometimes these issues can be sensitive and need to be handled by someone who is equipped to deal with them.

More often, though, an employee is demotivated at work because of external reasons. Maybe there is something the employee wants that he is not getting—better work conditions, a flexible schedule, the right to choose his coworkers or tasks. Is there any need or want you can tap into to give this employee more incentive to start working smarter, faster, and better?

Preparing for a Tough Conversation

Once you've diagnosed a persistent performance problem, you need to come up with a game plan for staging a purposeful intervention. This shouldn't be a dreaded confrontation doomed to be a terrible experience—it might be an intervention, but it should be a positive one.

First, review your notes from previous one-on-one meetings. Make sure you have all the pertinent details: dates and times that the employee has failed to take specific actions to meet the expectations you've been setting every step of the way. Second, consider your role in the employee's performance problem: Are you confident you've done a thoughtful and thorough job of trying to help this person improve? Did you spell out expectations clearly every step of the way? Did you monitor and measure fairly and accurately every step of the way? Have you given this person every opportunity to improve? Have you documented all of this clearly every step of the way? Before you proceed, consult an ally (or make a brand-new one) in HR. Make sure you are following proper procedures before you have this performance intervention.

If you've discussed the problem with the employee in the past and have done everything in your power to help the employee correct the problem, the confrontation should not come as a surprise to your employee. But you still need to prepare thoroughly. Create a script so you stay on track during the conversation. Anticipate any excuses the employee typically offers you for failing to improve performance. You've probably heard them all by now. By preparing, you'll be able to take a proactive approach to those excuses and address them before the person throws them at you again.

During the conversation, make sure you:

- Clarify that you are meeting to discuss a problem.

- Confront the employee in direct terms, letting her know that her failure to improve performance is unacceptable.

- Present the facts as you've documented them; be as specific as you can.

- Share a list of nonnegotiable action items that the person must complete within a specific schedule.

- Establish that failing to resolve the performance problem, whatever that might be, will result in negative consequences for the employee.

Negative Consequences

If an employee fails to improve his performance despite your regular coaching and putting him on warning, at some point, you simply have to follow through. You have to start imposing real negative consequences. What negative consequences can you impose?

- Stop going out of your way to help this employee meet her special needs and wants. Why should you go out of your way to take care of an employee who is chronically under-performing?

- Take away one or more special rewards the employee may have earned because of past performance. If the employee is not performing well anymore, why should she continue to enjoy these rewards? She is not earning them anymore. Always remind employees that rewards are not permanent but contingent on continued good performance.

- Use your discretion to punish the employee. For example, managers often have discretion when it comes to schedul-ing; why should the stubborn low performer be given the schedule she wants? Give her the worst schedule. Manag-ers also have a lot of discretion when it comes to assigning tasks. As one U.S. Army general put it to me once, "If a soldier has been dragging his heels all week, that soldier should have to clean the latrine next week. I always save the best duty assignments for the soldiers who are putting in the best effort and save the worst duty for the soldiers I want to punish a little."

Beyond these negative consequences, the only place to go is letting the employee know that his job is on the line. This is not quite firing yet. But warn the employee that if the performance problem is not corrected, he is in real imminent danger of being fired. Any wrong move on the part of the employee could be a ticket right out the door. Every time he makes a wrong move, you'll have to consider two options: Remove the person imme-diately or else give that person another chance.

Firing someone, of course, is the ultimate punishment. But before letting someone go, you should consider giving the employee one last chance. Why? There are five reasons.

1. You've already invested time, energy, and money in this person. If you invest a little bit more, then you might actually get a return on that investment.

2. Depending on the situation, the employee in question, and your own feelings about him, you may want to go the extra mile for the individual.

3. If you turn a low performer around, you will save the organization and your team the costs of turnover. These include the costs of removing an employee, including exit benefits; the costs of recruiting and training a replacement; and the costs of downtime that result from removing a staff person.

4. In the event of any dispute that results from firing someone, your case might be stronger if you have given the employee one last chance to improve performance before terminating him.

5. Your company may require it.

But there are also lots of good reasons why, at some point, the last chances have to stop. Here are the reasons.

1. If the person is hopeless, the costs of turnover are actually a fiction. The primary costs of the bad hire have already been incurred. Continuing to employ the person is a greater cost than losing her.

2. You shouldn't dedicate any more time, energy, and money to an employee you don't believe will improve with time.

3. Depending on the situation and the person, giving the direct report a last chance may simply offer her a chance to bad-mouth you, the team, and the organization; a chance to do bad work and cause problems; and a chance to steal or commit sabotage.

4. If you've kept accurate written records of your management interactions with this person and her failure to perform, then you probably don't need to give the person a last chance to strengthen your case. Your case is already strong.

5. Your company may require it.

Whether and when to fire an employee is always a tough decision. It's a business decision you have to make. If you've monitored, measured, and documented her performance every step of the way, you will be in a much better position to make the right decision.

Fire Stubborn Low Performers

Sometimes managers tell me, "I really want to fire an employee, but we are already understaffed and everybody on our team is already overworked. I feel as if I cannot fire my low performers because then the remaining employees will have to work even harder." These managers want to know, "Isn't a fifty percent performance from a low performer sometimes better than having no employee in that role at all?"

My answer to that is N-O. No, no, no!

There are, however, times when it makes sense to hold on to a stubborn low performer for a little while longer. If you are super busy, you might as well squeeze one last day of grunt work out of the low performer. As my clients in the restaurant industry are fond of saying, "Never fire the dishwasher on Friday night!" That's right. Have that low performer wash as many filthy dishes as you can get him to wash—all the worst pots and pans. And then fire him.

Choose your timing carefully. But you have to fire the low performers if they refuse to improve. Fifty percent of an employee is not better than zero. There are four reasons why you must fire stubborn low performers.

1. They get paid.

2. They cause problems that other employees have to fix.

3. High performers hate to work with low performers— and you can't afford to lose your high performers.

4. Low performers send a terrible message to everybody else: "Low performance is an option around here." No way. It shouldn't be an option.

If your team is overstaffed and overworked, then high performance is your only option. You have to be able to get more work and better work out of everyone. You cannot afford to have the negative energy and unnecessary problems of a stubborn low performer dragging down the rest of the team.

Firing an employee is one of the most unpleasant, scary things you'll ever have to do as a manager. But sometimes it just has to be done. You owe it to yourself, your team, and your organization. This is the extreme end of consequences in the workplace, but without hard consequences for persistent failure, accountability is meaningless.

Firing people is often not easy in an organization. You have to jump through hoops, usually, before you can fire someone. One of the reasons is fairness: everyone wants to make sure employees are not fired for reasons that have nothing to do with their job performance. And, of course, employers want to make sure they don't get sued by a fired employee or that they have done what's necessary to be able to successfully defend against a lawsuit, if one is brought up against them. Your organization has a process for firing an employee. Learn the rules. Follow the rules. Work the rules. And ask for help from your boss, other managers, HR, and your company's legal department.

If You Solve Problems Aggressively Every Step of the Way, You'll Probably Never Have to Fire Anyone

Still, sometimes it's almost impossible to fire an employee. Some organizations are so worried about being sued that they have an unwritten rule against firing. In other cases, the process for firing is so time-consuming and burdensome that managers feel that firing is just not a real option. I've had plenty of managers tell me that they spent huge chunks of time for months or even years trying to fire an employee. And sometimes, despite all that effort, the employee prevails and is not terminated. Indeed there are entire countries where the law actually makes it virtually impossible to fire an employee, or even demote one.

If you find yourself needing to get rid of an employee but stuck in one of these situations, what do you do? Pressure. Keeping up the intensity of your hands-on management and shining a bright light on their performance will usually be enough pressure to cause stubborn low performers to want to escape. Almost always, they will give up on you before you give up on them. Low performers don't like to be managed closely. They don't like scrutiny and don't like to incur consequences for their low performance. So manage that low performer very, very closely. Do everything in your power to impose consequences, however slight, for the person's low performance, every step of the way. Have you ever shined a bright light under a big rock? The vermin scamper away fast. If you shine a bright light on a low performer, he will usually start looking around for a way out. He'll go shopping for a manager who will leave him alone. He might move somewhere else in your organization. That, unfortunately, is no favor to the organization—but at least it solves the problem for you.

Of course, you should hope he finds a new job working for your competition.

CHAPTER 9

Do More for
Some People
and Less
for Others

You are struggling to complete the annual ranking of the twelve employees for whom you have reporting responsibility—a new requirement established by your company. There has been a lot of bad feeling and resentment about the new compensation system, and you are in a tough spot. If you use the maximum discretion you are allowed under the new system, you could give some people much bigger raises and bonuses and others much less. You know that you probably should do that, but you don't want to offend and anger the employees who would get less. There is little chance that the rankings and their financial consequences will remain a secret.

You single out two people—the two who are obvious superstars. You are allowed to give only two A ratings, but you don't give either employee an A+ rating because it would mean even bigger raises and bonuses, using up much of your discretionary pool. You are also required to give at least half your team Cs, so you split the team in half as best as you can. You are allowed to give C- and B+, but you don't give any—as it is, you know there will be bad feeling among the Cs, especially because they will get small raises and a zero annual cash bonus.

As you finish ranking your employees, you think to yourself, "My employees can't complain too much. After all, they receive good annual base salaries, good benefits, even a free membership to a gym. Everybody also gets a decent annual raise just for working here. It's a pretty good deal and the work conditions are not bad." Then Sam knocks on your office door and asks if you have a few minutes to discuss his work schedule. Sam doesn't want to work on Thursdays anymore. You look Sam in the eye and explain that Thursday is a busy day and that you can't let employees choose their own schedules, because if you did that for one, you'd have to do it for everybody. "I'm sorry, Sam. I can't make special deals with you. That wouldn't be fair to the other employees. There's nothing I can do. My hands are tied."

How is Sam likely to respond? That depends on what kind of employee Sam is, but here are the three most likely responses.

1. Sam might say, "I'm sorry I bothered you," and walk away quietly. But that's probably not what Sam is thinking. He is thinking, "That doesn't make any sense. Who cares about Thursdays except for me? After all I've done for you! Okay, let's see how much work I get done on Thursdays from now on ... and you probably won't even notice."

2. Sam might say, "I won't take no for an answer. You have to give me Thursdays off!" Maybe you'll tell Sam, "Too bad, go away." But what if Sam continues to insist? You might get mad and rush off an answer: "You don't talk to me like

that. I'm the boss. You're fired!" When you call HR, and they ask you if you have any documentation, you have to admit that Sam is a strong performer—and all the paper-work proves it. Now you and Sam are really at odds—and not just about Thursdays.

3. Sam might say, "Well, thanks for everything then, but I'm leaving. I've looked into my options in the free market for talent and there are some great employers out there. In fact, your competition across the street is going to give me Thursdays off. So I'm going across the street to work for them." If Sam is a high performer, he probably knows it and knows that he is worth more than a lower performer. He knows he is valuable.

    In this last scenario, you might tell Sam, "But I've worked with you and trained you, and now I really depend on you. You are a high performer, one of the employees I'd really hate to lose." Sam replies, "Exactly. That's what I was thinking. So how about giving me Thursdays off?"

Sam has a point. The truth that everybody knows but nobody likes to acknowledge is that one high-performing employee is worth more to the business than three or four mediocre em-ployees. Those high-performing employees know that they are valuable and want to use their value to earn what they need and want. The problem is that most pay-for-performance systems fail to do the hard work of ensuring high performance; this is tracked and linked directly to increased rewards. That hard work has to be done by managers on the front line who control the daily experience of employees and, ultimately, their access to rewards of all kinds.

If you are Sam's manager and you can't afford to lose him or be at odds with him, you might give in to his request. But you'd probably make the same mistake that a lot of managers make in this situation: you'd make a secret deal with Sam. "Okay, Sam, I'll let you have Thursdays off. But don't tell anybody." After employees catch on to your arrangement with Sam, Mary knocks on your door and says, "I understand that Sam doesn't have to work on Thursdays. He got to choose his own special schedule? Nobody else did! You are favoring Sam. That's not fair!"

You want to tell Mary, who is decidedly mediocre as an employee, "Fair? Do you want to know why I'm favoring Sam? Because Sam does more work than you do! He gets here early and leaves late and works hard the whole time he's here. He meets every deadline and takes exactly the right amount of initiative without overstepping his bounds. That's why Sam gets a special deal. Would you like me to favor you, too? Tell me what you need. Because there are a lot of things I need from you. I need you to start coming in earlier and working harder. I need you to start following procedures and getting tons of work done very well, very fast all day long. Do you want Thursdays off, too? Okay. Let's take it one Thursday at a time. If you want this Thursday off, here's what I need from you by this Wednesday at midnight. Let's spell out the expectations very clearly and let's write all that down."

I tell managers every single day: Don't make secret deals. Put a billboard in the parking lot: SAM DOESN'T HAVE TO WORK ON THURSDAYS. COME TO MY OFFICE TO FIND OUT WHY. Then deal with each person, one at a time, as each one knocks on your office door looking for a custom deal. You can't do everything for everybody, of course. And why would you want to? That wouldn't be fair. So you have to negotiate one employee at a time: "What do you need from me? Okay. Here's what I need from you."

The Dull Bludgeon of Treating Everybody the Same

Yet in the world of undermanagement, most managers gravitate to "sameness" because it's easier. Whether it's hourly pay or a fixed salary, when employees are paid according to a set system, the manager doesn't have to make and justify difficult decisions, or stay engaged with every employee by making sure she knows what to do to earn what she needs or wants. The manager is more comfortable when employees are rewarded based on a rigid structure, because she can answer her employees' queries by blaming the "system."

It is true that ease of administration, false fairness, and litigation avoidance are still the basic engines behind many compensation systems and HR policies. As much as forced ranking and pay for performance are creeping in, there is still a whole lot of nonperformance-based "sameness" in most organizations. Some of it is necessary. There are gym memberships or child care and other shared rewards that benefit all employees. They provide a feeling of belonging and connection to the company. They provide a sense of gratitude on the part of at least some employees. And they contribute to the well-being of employees, which probably creates better employees who provide a greater return on investment to the company over time. But by the time managers are done spending all their resources and discretion on treating everybody the same, there are very few resources left. I cannot tell you how many times managers tell me that they don't have sufficient resources to provide special rewards to high performers.

But when I dig down deeper, I find a lot of managers who hide behind "the system," even when they have much more discretion in the system than they actually use. Often managers have discretionary bonus pools and a lot of input on raises, but somehow everybody on the team shares in the bonus pool equally and everybody gets roughly the same raise. The same goes for work conditions and special accommodations. Managers often have a great deal of discretion when it comes to things like schedules, assigning tasks, setting work conditions, allocating supplies, and so on. So why do managers fail to favor some employees and pick on others? So many managers simply cannot or will not dedicate the time and energy necessary to make the tough performance-based distinctions and then follow through to reward people based on what they deserve.

Real Fairness

"High performers and low performers getting the same basic rewards? Now that's unfair," said one manager in a large manufacturing company. "You have to reward people based on what they deserve, based on what they earn."

Yes, you want to get more work and better work out of every employee. For their part, most employees are doing their best to succeed and are trying desperately to earn what they need and want. If you are going to do more for those who deserve more, by definition you must do less for those who deserve less. When they earn more, do more for them. When they earn less, do less for them. That's only fair.

Of course, you can't do everything for everybody. And why would you ever want to? Make clear who you are rewarding, how, and why. Maybe others will work hard to earn special rewards, too. That's why it's so important to make sure every employee knows how and why she is earning her rewards and what she needs to do in order to earn more (or less).

How do you do that? By defining expectations and tying concrete rewards directly to the fulfillment of those expectations. When every person on your team is managed this way, they are much less likely to wonder why another person is receiving special rewards. Why? Every single one of them knows from experience what they have to do to earn special rewards. They know that if Sam is receiving some special reward from you, he must have earned it fair and square. After all, that's the kind of manager you are.

If you tie rewards directly to behavior fairly, behavior will follow rewards.

Real Leverage

"The ability to do more, or less, for people is a source of great power." That's how one senior engineering manager, whom I'll call Hal, put it. Faced with a very important project and an urgent deadline, Hal had only one qualified engineer he could assign to work with him. "I needed [this] engineer to do the heavy lifting, basically to work around the clock for about three weeks. It was going to be brutal." When he approached Ginny, the engineer in question, Hal said, "she was hesitant to drop everything she was working on, get way behind on her work, and basically not see her family for a month. She couldn't exactly turn down the assignment, but I needed her on board and totally focused on completing the project at a really accelerated pace." After their initial conversation, Hal realized how much he was really asking of Ginny. So he went to his boss and got approval to offer Ginny a deal she couldn't refuse.

Hal continues, "I went back to Ginny and told her that we had to have her on board for this project. I offered to send home a letter to her family explaining the project and thanking them for their sacrifice. We would send a gift basket to the family, and we offered her a budget for the four weeks of the project to pay for extra child care. She really appreciated the thought we gave to her family. But the real hook was the money. We needed the project done in four weeks, as in twenty-eight days. So I offered Ginny a large cash bonus on day twenty-eight if the project was done. She was concerned that she might work really hard and miss the deadline by just one day, perhaps, and then not get any bonus at all." Here's what they finally agreed on. "Every day she was late, the cash bonus would diminish by ten percent. But she insisted on some upside to beating the deadline. I had to get that approved, but I was able to get her five percent more for every day she was early. In the end, she was six days early. She finished that project with all the bells and whistles in twenty-two days flat. She got this big bonus, plus an extra thirty percent." Now that's leverage.

Imagine if you could stop paying people and start buying their results, one by one. What do you think would happen if every manager had the discretion, the ability, the skill, and the gumption to start negotiating with employees as if they were outside vendors? What if you could tie every single reward and detriment solely to measurable instances of employee performance—one person at a time, one day at a time? Think of industries in which individuals are paid an agreed-upon amount for each defined unit of work they produce. Some accounting firms, for example, pay accountants per tax return they prepare or per audit; they pay more for more complex returns and audits, and they pay less when the reviewing accountant finds errors in the accountant's work. Some hotels pay chambermaids by the number of rooms they clean; some pay more per room if the rooms are cleaner, based on how well they complete a checklist of standards. Labor economists have convincing data that worker productivity increases substantially when pay is directly tied to performance. Why shouldn't this apply to all kinds of work?

Give every person the chance to meet the basic expectations of their jobs and then the chance to go above and beyond— and to be rewarded accordingly. Create trust and confidence through open communication and transparency so that every employee knows exactly what she has to do to earn rewards—no matter how great or small those rewards might be. Monitor and measure and document it every step of the way. Don't flinch when it comes to providing the promised rewards and detriments that people earn through their choices and behavior.

When your employees deliver on their commitments for you, you deliver on promised rewards for them. If they fail to meet commitments, you have to call them on that failure immediately and withhold the reward. Ideally, you want to reward people when they deliver results—no sooner, no later. Immediate rewards are most effective because there can be no doubt about the reason for the rewards, providing a greater sense of control and a higher level of reinforcement. Employees are likely to remember the precise details and context of the performance and are, therefore, better able to replicate the desired performance. Plus employees won't have to spend time wondering if their performance has been noted and appreciated and will therefore be less likely to lose the momentum generated by success.

Years ago, a cutting-edge business leader in the fitness equipment business I'll call Jon, told me that he looked at every front-line manager as a compensation officer. Jon created a culture in which managers rewarded performance constantly. "I really believe in spot bonuses. Every supervisor had authority to give bonuses to high performers, anywhere from a few hours pay to a week's pay. We had regular meetings with the supervisors and I would ask them, 'How many people did you give a bonus to last week?' If they hadn't given anybody a bonus, I'd say to them, 'Do you mean to tell me, you are managing forty people every week, and you couldn't find any reason to give somebody a bonus? What is the matter with you?' So these supervisors were always looking for reasons to give the guys on their crew spot bonuses." And you can be sure that the guys on the crew were doing backflips to be the ones who would earn those bonuses. It worked. Jon says: "In any given year, we were outproducing every other company in the industry with half the number of factory workers, and the spot bonuses were a huge part of that." When managers become de facto compensation officers, productivity explodes.

Be Generous and Flexible

"You want to be generous and flexible with your employees. Why wouldn't you? Everybody is working harder. Everybody is under more pressure. Everybody needs more than what they are getting." That's what Fred, a manager in charge of a public cafeteria, a food court, and convenience and retail gift stores at a large hospital, told me. "At the hospital, there just were not a lot of ways to reward my people. Most of them were paid by the hour. The salaried employees were on a pretty tight leash, too. For example, there was no paid time off."

This is where Fred turned from ordinary human being to Super Boss: "In my role as senior supervisor, I had accumulated unused sick days, personal days, and extra vacation days. You couldn't cash them in for money, but you could keep accumulating them. After twenty years, I had a couple of hundred days I had never used, and the reality was that I just wasn't going to use them any time soon. I couldn't just disappear for weeks at a time, and I was getting thirty days a year or something by then anyway. So I asked HR if I could start handing out my days to individual employees as rewards. The HR specialist was trying to convince me to rethink. He told me that if I had enough days at the end of my career there, I might be able to arrange a whole year of paid time off ... I didn't have to think about it again ... I was finally able to get them to agree, at least in part. They let me give away twenty-five days a year, which is about two days a month.... That lasted for about four years, and then someone upstairs put a stop to it. But for those four years, I had that great reward in my back pocket all the time and people knew it. And boy, did they appreciate getting those paid days off," Fred said with a smile of satisfaction.

If you are the boss, one of the most important parts of your job is taking care of your people. Remember, people work to take care of themselves and their families. They want your help. Some managers consistently do more for their employees. If you're not one of those managers, what is your problem?

Start looking at the discretionary resources that are within your disposal already. Use your power over work conditions; scheduling; recognition; exposure to decision makers; deciding what tasks are assigned to whom, who gets extra training opportunities, where each employee works, and with what coworker; and so on. In my view, if you have a candy jar on your desk and an employee goes reaching for a piece of chocolate, you should stop that person in his tracks and say, "So, you want a piece of chocolate? Here's what I need from you, by this deadline, and here are the guidelines. Do you understand?"

Have you gone to great lengths to extend your discretionary resources? Get on the phone and beg for more resources, jump through hoops, and bend over backward if you have to. Use whatever resources you can get your hands on as bargaining chips to drive performance and to reward people when they go the extra mile. What are the key elements of every job that employees typically care about, that are often within the discretion of the manager, and that can be used as bargaining chips to drive performance?

The compensation package. What is the base pay and the value of the benefits? How much of the pay is fixed? How much is contingent on clear performance benchmarks tied directly to concrete actions the individual employee can control? What are the levers for driving the pay up or down?

Schedule. What is the default schedule? How much flexibility is there? What are the levers for achieving more or less scheduling flexibility?

Relationships. Who will the employee be working with? Which vendors, customers, coworkers, subordinates, and managers? What are the levers for controlling who the employee has a chance to work with (and/or avoid)?

Tasks. Which regular tasks and responsibilities will the employee be assigned to do? Are there any special projects? What are the levers for controlling the employee's opportunities to work on more choice tasks, responsibilities, or projects?

Learning opportunities. What basic skills and knowledge will the employee be learning in order to handle his basic tasks and responsibilities? Will there be any special learning opportunities? What are the levers for controlling access to those special learning opportunities?

Location. Where will the employee be located? How much control will the employee have over his workspace? Will there be much travel? Are there opportunities to be transferred to other locations? What are the levers for controlling these location issues?

Help People Earn What They Need and Want

Every employee wants a custom deal that includes some or all of these key elements of the job. They want to know what they need to do to earn more in each of these areas. Help people by telling them exactly what they need to do to earn more.

When an employee says, "I don't want to work on Thursday," tell her she needs to do A, B, and C by Wednesday at midnight. You are giving the employee control over her rewards by spelling out exactly what she needs to do to earn them. You'll have to monitor, measure, and document that the employee completed A, B, and C by Wednesday at midnight. If she has, you'll have the opportunity to reward her in a very powerful way. Using your power over scheduling flexibility, you will get more work from that employee faster and also provide her with an immediate reward that is valuable to her. In fact, it has unique value for her precisely because she wanted it in particular.

Why? Because when you find out what a particular employee really needs or wants from you, it is like finding a needle in a haystack. As one manager told me, "A big part of the art of rewarding is knowing who to reward with what, when, and how. It's different for every person. One of my employees needs to leave once in a while to deal with her kids, usually at the last minute with no warning. I let her do that because I know how valuable it is to her. But the flip side is that she is always working really hard to make sure I know she appreciates the flexibility. She has told me plenty of times that this flexibility is what makes the job work for her. She appreciates it so much that she works doubly hard to make sure I really know she deserves the accommodation. And I do, I really do think she deserves it. She earns it every day." When you identify an employee's "needle [or needles] in a haystack," you've identified a powerful bargaining chip. The employee will probably be willing to do a lot—to work longer, harder, smarter, faster, or better—in order to get it.

I always tell managers that when your employees make unreasonable demands, don't be insulted—be grateful. They are telling you exactly what they want. They are handing you that needle in a haystack. It's so much harder when you have to look for it on your own. If you can find a way to offer this needle in a haystack, then you are in a position to make a custom deal with this individual.

Let me tell you my best needle-in-a-haystack story. Nat, a

manager for a large U.S. intelligence agency that employs high-level mathematicians, hired a young PhD from a prestigious university. The young man began working as an analyst, but very quickly, according to Nat, "he was moping around, not talking to anybody, not really doing as much work as he should have been doing. He seemed almost depressed." Nat tried to engage the new employee, by talking with him one-on-one. "I could tell that this guy had a fantastic mind and a great interest in the work, but he was frustrated and something was bothering him. Finally, he told me it was his workspace: 'I can't work here in this cubicle at this desk. It ruins it for me. I need my thinking couch.'" Nat laughed, "The guy basically said, 'I can't do math without my couch.'" The analyst explained to Nat that he had a couch in his apartment around which he had his computers arranged on tables. He had apparently had the couch for a number of years, having written his undergraduate honors thesis, studied for all of his exams in college and graduate school, and written his doctoral dissertation sitting on that couch. The new analyst was very attached to the experience of working on that couch.

Regardless of whether this was a small quirk or a huge obsessive-compulsive anomaly, Nat considered the analyst's rather unusual request. "At first I said no," Nat explained. "Where would we put the couch? But the analyst had measured it and showed me that it would fit right in the cubicle. We had to take out his chair and trade his desk for a table. We had the couch tested for bomb residue and had dogs sniff it for explosives. We even provided the movers. We let him set up his office just the way he wanted it, including his MP3 player, his two computers, and his bookshelf filled with binders and books. And from that moment on, he was the happiest employee here

that I know. He's here all the time, as far as I know ... I think he
sleeps on that couch. He never leaves."

Make a point of talking with your best people to find out
what they really want or need—whether it's a special deal or a
small accommodation. If you can fulfill a unique need or want,
you will be doing something especially valuable for that person.
When you need extra leverage with a particular employee—
when you need her to really go the extra mile—there is no better motivational tool than using her "needle in a haystack" as a
bargaining chip.

How do you make those needles work for you as supersonic
bargaining chips? Leverage them for everything they are
worth.

- "You don't want to work on Thursday? I'm glad to know
  that. Here's what I need from you by Wednesday at midnight."

- "You want your own office? Here's what I need from you."

- "You want to bring your dog to work? Great. Here's what I
  need from you."

- "You want to have lunch with the senior VP? Here's what I
  need from you."

Expand your repertoire of rewards and start using every resource you have to drive performance.

Of course, some rewards are just not available. Sometimes,
as much as you want to make a custom deal with an employee,
you have to say, "I just can't do that. It's not available. But maybe
I can do this instead." It's not ideal, but it's better than saying,

"There's nothing I can do for you." We've learned from experience that when managers really put their creativity and energy into it, they can often do more than they ever would have
guessed. If you are willing to jump through hoops, bend over
backward, and go to bat for what you need, you'll find that you
can often get resources and be able to make custom deals with
employees that you never thought would be available. Use those
custom deals to drive performance every step of the way.

Use Your Discretion Wisely

The corollary to making custom deals for hardworking employees is the case in which an employee makes accommodations for
himself without your prior approval. Often managers will say to
me, "I have an employee who is excellent and very valuable. But
… he is fifteen minutes late every day" or "wears inappropri-
ate clothing" or "makes a lot of personal calls" and on and on.
These managers often say, "I've been letting this small problem
slide because the employee is otherwise so valuable."

When a manager lets an otherwise high-performing employee off the hook on a small performance issue, the manager
is making a custom deal—offering an informal reward—
without even realizing it. If this is the case with you, first decide
whether you've been letting a performance problem slide because the employee obviously appreciates this informal reward.
You might use your discretion and continue to allow the special
accommodation, but you must make it explicit and, if appropriate, even a formal custom deal. Sit down with the employee
and explain: "Doing X is actually kind of a problem. It's been
bothering me. But I've been letting it slide because you are such

a great employee in every other way. Just how important is this to you? I want to talk about it because you need to know that I am letting the problem slide as a special reward." Clarify that there are other rewards the employee might earn instead of this special accommodation, or that you are offering this custom deal because there are so few other formal rewards you can offer the person. Whatever it is, don't let it slide. Make the quid pro quo explicit.

It's also critical that employees know that custom deals are not to be taken for granted and always remain contingent on your discretion. "I've learned to stay away from long-term promises," said Winny, a manager in a large nonprofit organization with tight resource constraints. "Things are changing all the time. You realize that someone might not be quite the employee you had thought he was or hoped he would be … Once you give someone a raise, or a promotion, or a special schedule, or an office, it's hard to take it back," said Winny. "Once you make a special deal with someone, you might get into a situation where you have to start doing takeaways, and that can get ugly. So I stick to onetime rewards. Lots of onetime rewards."

Winny continued, "When I took over this location, every employee had his own special deal. I mean everyone, including the people who didn't do a thing. As one of my staff said about a coworker, 'She doesn't belong on the payroll. She doesn't do any work whatsoever.'" And yet she was on the payroll, and she was welcome to the free doughnuts and coffee that were brought in every morning for the employees and lunch on Fridays. She was invited to the monthly pizza night for employees and the annual holiday party. Plus, she got the $200 gift certificates as a holiday bonus, just like the other employees. All of these perks were paid for out of an employee reward fund, which was made available to the manager of the location.

"The employee reward fund wasn't much," explained Winny, "about $5,000 all together. When they announced that money was available to each location, the manager who was here before me held a meeting and asked the team how they thought the money should be spent." Some had argued that the money should be split evenly among all the employees, but the manager resisted this, apparently not wanting to hand out cash bonuses to some of the people who were undeserving. So the manager came up with the idea of spreading the money around while also investing in team-building activities, like the lunches, parties, and shared doughnuts and coffee. "The first thing I did when I took over was to change that system. I was going to figure out how to spend the reward fund in a way that was fair and use it to make some things happen. In the end, I used that money almost entirely for spot bonuses. A hundred bucks at a time. People wanted to earn those cash bonuses. They'd ask me, 'What do I have to do to earn one of those bonuses?' So I'd say, 'Funny you should ask … '"

Everything Is Negotiable (Almost)

Employment relationships are transactional by nature. If you want to get the work done very well and very fast on favorable terms, you have to be very good at negotiating all the terms—schedule, location, resources, and compensation. Is the deadline going to be March 1, or March 15? Will there be bonuses for early delivery or exceptional quality? Penalties for late delivery or work that fails to meet expectations? The ideal bargain is one that clearly defines the deliverables expected and a concrete deadline, as well as specific milestones that need to be reached along the way. Every penny of compensation—financial and nonfinancial—would be tied either to a specific milestone in the project or to the ultimate delivery by the agreed-upon deadline. In an ideal world, if at any point an employee fails to deliver, she doesn't get paid.

Does that mean that everything is open to negotiation? Of course not. In fact, if you are going to get good at negotiating with employees, the first thing you have to consider is what is *not* negotiable. What are the basic requirements of the job, the essential performance standards, and acceptable behavior? What are the basics for which employees should expect nothing more than to be treated fairly and paid for their work? Those are your deal breakers. You have to be very clear with your employees and remind them on a regular basis: "Okay. Here's the deal. For coming in to work on time, for not leaving early, and for getting a lot of work done very well all day long without causing any problems, you get paid. And you get to keep working here!" Those are the basics of the employment deal. Your employees should understand that doing their jobs very well, very fast, all day long is what they were hired to do. That's why they get paid a basic wage or salary. That's why they get the basic benefits. That's why they all get to come to the pizza party.

Once you figure out what is *not* negotiable, you have to accept and embrace the fact that everything—and I mean everything—else is negotiable. Don't be alarmed. Don't your employees negotiate with you all the time on matters of all shapes and sizes? Take control of the ongoing negotiation. Negotiate every step of the way and get really, really good at it. That means constantly answering the questions that are on every employee's mind: "What's the deal around here? What do you want from me? And what do I get for my hard work ... today, tomorrow, and next week?" Beyond the basic employment deal, employees should know that if they need or want more, they have to earn those rewards through their own hard work.

Understand, accept, and embrace that managing people has become a day-to-day negotiation. Abandon your top-down assumptions of hierarchical leadership and let go of your insult. It's a job! Employment relationships are transactional. You are the boss. You want to get more and better work faster out of every employee. Meanwhile, your employees work to earn a living and want to get more rewards in exchange for their hard work. Whom do they look to? You, the boss. They should have trust and confidence that you will do your best to help them earn those rewards. The only way you can honor that trust and confidence is by doing more for some people and less for others.

CHAPTER 10

Start Here

You just finished reading this book, *It's Okay to Be the Boss* ... Well, you are almost done reading it. But you've already decided to become a much better boss. You are ready—eager even—to start managing in a more hands-on manner. You start meeting with your employees, one-on-one, just like the book says. In fact, you are going to meet with everybody this morning. You have a notebook under your arm, ready to take notes. Of course, you haven't been managing very closely up to this point, so your new approach takes your employees a little by surprise. They're murmuring to each other, "What's going on?" But one savvy employee chimes in, "Haven't you noticed? He's been walking around with that book, *It's Okay to Be the Boss*, all week. He's obviously trying some new management fad. Don't worry. This will blow over soon." The other employees start smiling and nodding with relief (and a tiny bit of disappointment), echoing, "Right. This will blow over. Just ignore it."

Will it blow over or not? That's entirely up to you.

Maybe you are inspired to become a better boss. You make real changes, managing more closely for a while, but then reality sets in. You are incredibly busy and realize that managing more closely is time consuming, especially at first. Perhaps some employees push back and complain that you are micromanaging or picking on them, or favoring some more than others. There has been a lot of tension in the air, so you get heat from your boss, who is not happy that you've "upset the apple cart," as he put it. "You can't just come in one day and say I'm changing every-thing around here. No more Mr. Nice Guy." Everyone thinks you are being too harsh, and it's clear your new approach isn't going well. You start to wonder if you are just not good at this. After all, you've never been a natural leader. So you find your-self backing away from your new approach, quickly and steadily until you are back to the status quo ante.

"Phew! I'm glad that's over," you might think as you go back to the familiar routine of hands-off management, in which the problems are many and deep, but at least you don't see them coming in advance. They strike by surprise and you run around, acting like Mr. Jerk Boss while trying to solve the problem. It's a huge, unpleasant hassle, but at least when it's over, everyone can go back to being disengaged until the next unnecessary cri-sis erupts. In the meantime, you and everyone else can enjoy going back to Mr. False Nice Guy Friend.

This Decision Is Too Important to Rush

Throughout this book, I've tried desperately to convince you to become a better boss. That is my mission: to persuade manag-ers like you to dedicate yourself to being strong, disciplined, and all about the work. I want you to start holding your em-ployees accountable and helping all of them work harder to earn what they need every day. I want you to get in there and start managing. But first, you have to take a giant step back.

Today's workplace is high pressure and today's workforce is high maintenance—managing is getting harder and harder. Think, think, think: Are you ready, willing, and able to commit the time, energy, effort, and consistency that it will take to change? Are you prepared to become a great boss? Your role at work is going to change. Your relationships at work are going to change. Your experience at work is going to change. You are going to be the person who is all about the work, who is setting people up for success every day, who is helping every person earn what she needs. That's going to be you from now on.

Consider the Culture of Your Workplace

Before making a big change in your approach to managing, think about the culture of your workplace. Does the culture support hands-on management? Or is everybody else around here pretty hands-off? What will it mean for you, in the context of this corporate culture, to become a very strong, highly engaged, transactional, coaching-style boss? Will you fit right in? Or will this make you something of a maverick?

Sometimes managers tell me, "This organization is very conservative. We don't believe in confrontation. We don't like to rock the boat . . . So the culture is very hands-off management." Just as often managers tell me, "This organization is very progressive. We let employees do their own thing. We don't like to boss people around . . . So the culture is very hands-off."

Sometimes managers say, "Our organization is very large and there is lots of red tape and bureaucracy . . . So the culture is hands-off." Other managers say, "Our organization is very small and there is more of a family dynamic in the workplace ... So the culture is hands-off."

Or else, "Our work is very technical ... So the culture is hands-off." Or, "Our work is very creative ... So the culture is hands-off."

Or else, "Our employees are much older ... So the culture is hands-off." Or, "Our employees are much younger ... So the culture is hands-off."

Or, "Our employees do low-level grunt work ... So the culture is hands-off." Or, "Our employees are all high-level professionals ... So the culture is hands-off management ..."

You get the idea. Think about it. Corporate culture is the combined web of shared meaning and shared social practices that develop between and among people in an organization. Remember? There is an undermanagement epidemic throughout the workplace, at all levels in organizations of all shapes and sizes. So of course most corporate cultures support a hands-off status quo in which strong managers often feel like ducks out of water. What can you do about it?

Be different.

And don't keep it a secret. Let people know. Stand out as the manager who is serious about the work and always goes the extra mile when it comes to managing. If being strong makes you a maverick in your particular organization, be a maverick. Being the maverick can be uncomfortable. Do it anyway. Be the manager who is not afraid to be the boss. Be the manager who is strong. Be hands-on.

I remember in the eighth grade, a year when I was more apt than not to be misbehaving, one of my teachers was really tough. Mr. Benson, my English teacher, was kind of a maverick among the other teachers. He was an intense guy and very strict. He gave pop quizzes all the time and made us write one book report after another. I remember trying harder and learning more in his class than in any other that year. Mr. Benson once ripped up my paper on *Johnny Tremain* because I had failed to dot my "i's." What a beautiful metaphor for quality control. Ever since then and to this day, I've always dotted my "i's" with a star—anyone who has ever seen my written hand can attest to that.

I can't remember any of my other teachers from the eighth grade, but I've never forgotten Mr. Benson.

Be that person.

You might find out that the culture supports good management after all. There may be more hands-on managers in your midst than you realize, doing their thing beneath the radar. Or you may find that your example is an inspiration to others.

Deciding to become a strong manager is a big step. If you think you are ready, commit to making permanent changes and remind yourself of that decision often. You'll be surprised at how much that helps.

Prepare

Then, before going public, prepare yourself to change your management approach.

- Set aside one hour a day for managing.

- Practice talking like a performance coach.

- Create a manager's landscape.

- Make a preliminary schedule.

- Set up a performance tracking system.

Set Aside That One Hour a Day for Managing

The first thing you should do is get in the habit of managing every day. But you don't actually need to start managing people just yet. Find the one hour a day that works best for you, and set it aside every day for two weeks before you actually plunge into managing employees in one-on-one sessions. During those two weeks, use this one hour a day to prepare.

Start by gathering information and tuning in informally to your employees and their work. Stop talking about everything under the sun with your employees and start talking about the work. And ask more questions: "Hey, what are your priorities today? What are you planning to do on plan X today? What steps do you normally follow to do task X? How long do you think that will take?" At the end of the day, ask people: "Hey, what did you focus on today? How far did you get on task X?"

When you are informally tuning in, you don't need to say too much. Just listen; you'll find some surprises. Some people will be put off that you are even asking. That's a good sign that you've been too hands-off until now. Some people will give vague answers. Others will tell you more than you would have guessed. You will start to learn who is doing what, where, why, when, and how. Just listen and make some notes to yourself. Remember, at this stage, you are just gathering information.

Practice Talking Like a Coach

As you are talking more and more with your employees about the work, practice talking like a performance coach.

- Tune in to the individual you are coaching.

- Focus on specific instances of individual performance.

- Describe the person's performance honestly and vividly.

- Focus on concrete next steps and describe them vividly.

Of course, it takes a while to get good at talking like a coach. But you might as well practice that way of talking as you start to build the habit of managing for an hour every day.

Create Your First Manager's Landscape

Do you remember the manager's landscape tool I described in chapter 4? This is the tool for tuning in to each employee so that you can customize your approach to managing that person. Before you plunge in and start holding regular one-on-one management conversations with each employee, create a landscape. Lay out the six questions across a piece of paper:

Who? | Why? | What? | How? | Where? | When?

Then fill out each column by considering each question carefully.

Who is this person at work? What do I know about this person that is relevant to work? Where is she coming from and where is she going?

Why do I need to manage this person? What does this person need from me to succeed at this job? What matters to this person? What do I need from this person? What matters to me with respect to this person in this job?

What should I be talking about with this person? Should I be focusing on larger goals or small goals? Broad guideline or detailed guidelines? Reminders of basic standard operating procedures or ideas about innovation?

How should I be talking with this person? Should we be talking through the work to be done step-by-step? Or should we just go over the big picture of the assignment? Should I be giving instructions? Or should I be asking questions? Should I be stern or warm?

Where? What location is the best to meet? If the person is in a remote location, how are we going to make the phone and e-mail work?

When? Should I check in several times a day with her or is once every other day or once a week enough? When is the best time to talk to her?

At this stage, remember, you are still making educated guesses. Your first manager's landscape is only a starting point. But you have to start somewhere. Over time, as you start managing people more closely, you will get more and more tuned in; and as circumstances and people change, expect to revisit these questions and answers again and again. If you have a lot of people to manage, the process will be time consuming. But no matter how many people you manage, this is where you begin to appreciate the challenge ahead of you, to tune in to your employees, and to customize your approach to managing each of them.

Revise your manager's landscape often. It's going to be an important tool for the rest of your management career.

Make a Preliminary Schedule for Managing People

Based on your manager's landscape, you should be able to make a preliminary schedule to begin your one-on-one management sessions.

Start thinking about when you are going to meet with whom and for how long. If you've been using one hour a day to prepare for this change in your management practices, then you are well on your way to making that "hour-a-day management" a habit. Now you need to decide how you are going to divide that time among your employees. During the initial meetings, you may have to dedicate more time than one hour a day, perhaps even an hour and a half per day, until your one-on-one meetings become routine and brief. At first, plan to schedule two or three one-on-one meetings per day. Can you get to every employee on your team in one week? Is that a feasible time commitment? If so, create a preliminary schedule.

Your schedule will take shape gradually as you start managing closely. Thereafter, you will probably negotiate times with each person on an ongoing basis. What's critical is that you schedule time with every person every week, if possible. What's even more critical is that they become your number one time commitment. Once you schedule one-on-one management meetings, they are sacrosanct.

But you're not quite ready to start holding one-on-one meetings just yet. Put that schedule on the back burner for a little while longer ...

Set Up a Performance Tracking System

Before you can plunge in to one-on-one management conversations, you need to have a practical system for tracking employees' performance. It doesn't have to be the best tracking system in the world. You are going to revise and adjust it with use over time until it becomes first-rate. But on day one, you need to have something in place. How are you going to monitor, measure, and document each employee's performance? What kind of approach seems to fit each person you manage? Will you need a separate tracking system for each employee, or will the same tracking system work for everyone? Will it be on paper or electronic? Will it be a notebook you carry around in your back pocket or a big binder that you carry around under your arm? What format are you going to use?

The most important thing about your tracking system is that you come up with a system that you will actually use, a system that works for you, that you can stick to. The sooner you figure that out, the better.

Go Public

Now that you've prepared mentally and have a schedule and a tracking system in place, it's time to go public and start discussing the impending management changes with the key people you depend on at work.

You don't want to act as if you've been failing as a manager until now. Instead adopt a more simple message: "I'm going to be a better manager, and here's what that means." Before you announce your intentions to your employees, you need to reach out to some key players. As you have these initial conversations, remember that this is good news. You are not announcing that you are going to start acting like a jerk. You are announcing that you are going to be on the path to becoming a great boss. You are going to be spending more time setting people up for success. You are going to provide more guidance and direction and support. You are going to help your employees do better, work smarter and faster, suffer fewer problems, and earn more rewards. That is good news! Make sure you feel that so it guides your tone in these initial conversations.

First, Talk to Your Boss

Most bosses will be delighted to hear that you want to work hard to become a better manager and will be happy to help you in your efforts. If your boss is going to be an obstacle, you'd better find out immediately.

First, spell out for your boss exactly what you are trying to accomplish. Second, ask your boss if she supports your efforts. Explain that you need her help and guidance. Third, be honest with her and talk about coming up with some standard operating procedures to guide you and your boss as you work on this together. Does your boss have different standards and requirements for your employees than you do? If so, decide with your boss which standards are going to be required of employees. Whatever standards you decide on, you and your boss should be requiring the same ones.

Does your boss go around you to interact directly with your employees? If so, decide together whether that is going to continue. Agree on ground rules for when and where and how each of you will meet with the employees who report to you. Agree on what you will discuss with those employees and what your boss will handle. If you plan on discussing similar things with your employees, agree to talk regularly to ensure you are both conveying the same messages to your direct report.

Do your employees go around you to your boss when they should be dealing directly with you? If so, decide with your boss exactly how the two of you are going to deal with this. In some cases, if employees try to end-run you, your boss can walk the employee back to your office so the three of you can discuss the matter together. Your boss can let you handle the matter and chime in to support you.

You don't need permission from your boss to be strong, talk like a coach, spend an hour a day managing, customize your approach to each person, tell people what to do and how to do it, track performance every step of the way, or identify and solve small problems before they turn into big problems. But you could definitely use your boss's help when it comes to holding employees accountable, imposing negative consequences on low performers, and helping high performers earn special rewards.

If your boss doesn't believe in hands-on management, buy her a copy of this book. At least persuade her to accept and support what you are trying to do—even just some of it. If you are not able to persuade her, smile and be strong anyway. If your boss is as hands-off as she's telling you to be, she will have a hard time holding you accountable for her poorly conceived directions. Meanwhile, the results on your team will likely improve, the disgruntled low performers will go away, and the rest of your team will likely be much happier. The results will speak volumes and might cause your boss to reconsider. At the same time, you'll be honing your management skills and building a strong track record in case you have to go shopping for a new boss who understands and accepts strong hands-on management.

After you talk to your boss, consider other key partners and colleagues you need to apprise of any coming changes. Think about how the changes are going to affect the people with whom you interact routinely and who interact routinely with your employees. Whomever you need to prepare or enlist, sit down and talk with them, one by one. Tell them your plan. Ask for their support.

Once you've had these preliminary conversations with your boss and other key people, you should be pretty warmed up.

START HERE   175

With any luck, you are even more committed already as a result of these conversations.

Talk to Your Team

If you already have a regular team meeting, at some point you need to announce to your team, "I'm going to be a better manager, and here's what that means." What if you don't have a regular team meeting? Are you going to call people together for the sole purpose of announcing this big change in your management style and practices? Is it really that big of a deal? I think it is.

Get everybody together, and in the full light of public disclosure make a commitment to yourself and your team. Even if you decide that a team meeting is not a good idea, and instead talk to each of your employees separately about the impending changes, the message should be the same: "I am going to be a better manager. Here's what that means: I'm going to work more closely with you. I'm going to spend an hour every day meeting with you all in one-on-one meetings for fifteen minutes or so—at least once a week. I'm going to try really hard to set every one of you up for success every step of the way. I will spell out expectations more clearly and provide more planning tools and checklists. I will track performance more closely so that I can provide more guidance, direction, and support. I will work hard to help you solve small problems before they turn into big ones. And I will work hard to help every one of you earn more of what you need and want. Are you with me?"

Be prepared for your employees to be concerned, to ask lots of questions, to second-guess you, and to doubt that you will follow through. It will take them a while to get used to it. A good way to end the team meeting is to schedule your initial one-on-one meeting with each person on the team.

There's Nothing Left to Do but Start Managing . . . One Person at a Time, One Day at a Time

If you've done all the necessary preparations, you are ready to start a regular schedule of ongoing one-on-one management conversations with every person you manage.

Before each initial meeting, prepare by going over your manager's landscape.

Write a script that reiterates your commitment to becoming a better manager and emphasizes what your new management relationship will look like. Explain that this is a learning process for you and that you will make mistakes. Explain that you plan to revise and adjust your approach as you go forward. Let the person know that you understand this is a big change for her, too, and that you expect her to go through a learning process. Explain that you need her help in making this change work for both of you. Explain that you know you will get better and better at this new relationship, and so will she.

After you've talked about why you are making this big change, the most important thing to discuss is the parameters of your regular management conversation. How often will you meet with this person? Exactly when and for how long? Where? Make sure the person understands that you are 100 percent committed to this new approach, but that you are also flexible. The best way to end this initial meeting is to reiterate your plans for the next meeting: When? Where? How long? What will you talk about?

The first meetings are likely to be awkward. That's okay. Over time, you and the people you manage will get better and better at using the meetings to get what you need from each other. Remember, this will be a moving target. Keep revisiting the questions in your manager's landscape. And keep talking about the work. Talk like a performance coach. Describe, describe, describe. Break it down. Focus on next steps. Describe, describe, describe. Break it down some more. In future meetings, prepare before each meeting by reviewing your notes from the last meeting in your tracking system. Take notes *during* the meeting and transcribe them into your tracking system *after* the meeting.

Remember the old rule of schoolteachers? Start off very strict and then, after the students come to expect, accept, and adapt to the strict regime, you can relax a bit. As long as the students continue to act as if they are still in the strict regime, you don't have to be quite as strict. The same basic rule applies to managing employees, but you have to do it one person at a time.

Start out intensely hands-on and you'll figure out immediately how closely each person needs to be managed and how you need to calibrate your management approach. Alert the employee that you have high expectations and, as she delivers on those expectations, you can gradually back off. If the employee keeps delivering, back off some more. But keep meeting regularly to review priorities, clarify expectations, and monitor, measure, and document that person's performance.

If an employee's performance falters in any way, tighten the reins for a while. If an employee slows down, starts missing details or deadlines, or engages in unacceptable behavior, be more hands-on for a while. If there is a big change in circumstances, such as the employee is assigned a new role, task, or responsibility, be more hands-on for a while. Be more hands-on until you have things under control. Then you can back off just a little bit again.

"How Am I Supposed to Respond to That?" Employee Push-backs and Strong Manager Responses

During your first one-one-one management meetings, or whenever you start managing employees hands-on, some of them are likely to push back. As soon as you try to hold employees accountable for their actions, some will surely come back with excuses. In fact, when you ask employees to "account for" their actions, some employees seem to come up with every retort under the sun. What are managers to say? Here are a few ways to respond to the classic employee push-backs.

Employee push-back: "Don't tell me how to do my job; don't micromanage me. I know what I'm doing; don't you trust me?"

Manager's response: "I need to understand exactly what you are doing and exactly how you are doing it. And I need to make sure you are doing exactly what I need you to do exactly how I need you to do it. So let's talk through exactly what you are going to do and exactly how you are going to do it, step-by-step."

Employee push-back: "It's not my fault."

Manager's response: "Let's look at exactly what you did, when, and how, step-by-step. And let's look at the results."

Employee push-back: "It's not fair."

Manager's response: "Let's talk about what you think would be fair and why that would be fair. But first let's talk about exactly what consequences you are unhappy with, and let's look at what actions caused those consequences."

Employee push-back: "What about me? I want _____."

Manager's response: "You want _____? I'm so glad to know that. Let's talk about exactly what you would have to do to earn that."

Employee push-back: "You don't have the facts."

Manager's response: "I have the following facts. Here's exactly what I know. Tell me what facts I don't have. Tell me where those facts are coming from."

Employee push-back: "The assignment is flawed."

Manager's response: "The assignment is not flawed for the following reasons. Let me tell you again what to do and how to do it." Or "You are right, the assignment is flawed. Now here is what you can do to accomplish most of the assignment anyway, even with the flaws."

Employee push-back: Stonewalling. (No response or very minimal response. Example: arms crossed, no words.)

Manager's response: "We have to be able to talk about your work and how you are doing it." Then ask direct questions. Start with a series of yes or no questions. Continue with narrow questions calling for brief answers. Gradually move on to slightly broader questions. If the stonewalling returns, return to yes or no and other narrow questions.

Employee push-back: "Yes, yes, yes, yes, yes," or "You are right, you are right, you are right."

Manager's response: "Thank you. I'm glad you agree. Now let's define concrete next steps so we can measure success or failure." Break up the next steps into small tasks and monitor them closely. You have to follow up the "Yes, yes, yes" with an immediate track record of success for that person or else an immediate track record of failure. If the track record following "Yes, yes, yes" is failure, then you respond to the next "Yes, yes, yes" with incredulity. You say, "We had this conversation yesterday. You said, 'Yes, yes, yes,' but you didn't do what we agreed. So 'Yes, yes, yes' is not a sufficient response. It can be interpreted as 'Leave me alone, please,' and that response is unacceptable."

Employee push-back: "You're picking on me."

Manager's response: "I'm so glad you noticed. Let me tell you exactly why I am picking on you … "

Employee push-back: "You favor Mary."

Manager's response: "Let me tell you why I go out of my way to reward Mary. Because she does more work than other people. When I ask her to do something, she does it. When I don't ask her to do something, she figures out what to do and does it. Do you want me to go out of my way for you? Let me tell you exactly what I need you to do. Let's set clear goals with clear guidelines and concrete deadlines. Meet those goals within those guidelines by these deadlines, and I'll start going out of my way for you."

Stay Flexible: Revise and Adjust Every Step of the Way

After you start managing people closely for six weeks or so, the nuances of your management challenge will become increasingly clear. You will have a better idea of who is doing what, where, why, when, and how. You've gotten over the surprises. You've done a lot of adjusting. Your meetings with each person will start to feel like standard operating procedure. If you've been monitoring, measuring, and documenting each person's performance in your tracking system, then you will have accumulated a written record of patterns for each person.

Once you've had a chance to digest what's going on and given your new management style a chance to work its wonders (usually six weeks is enough time to see some big results), you will naturally get to a point where some decisions are obvious: You need to fire Sam. You need to make sure you don't lose Chris. You need to shift around certain tasks and responsibilities from Pat to Bobby. And you should probably meet with Pat every day for a while, but you need to meet with Bobby only once a week.

Whatever those decisions may be, you have to trust the process. Take action. Don't slow down. Don't get stuck. Stay flexible. Be prepared to revise and adjust every step of the way as circumstances and people change. Keep meeting regularly with every person. Keep monitoring and measuring and documenting. Continue to revisit your manager's landscape regularly. Keep asking yourself:

- Who needs to be managed more closely? Who needs a little more space?

- Who is likely to improve? Who is not?

- Who should be developed? Who should be fired?

- Who are your best people? Who are your real performance problems?

- Who requires special accommodations and rewards? Who deserves them?

How to Manage Employees Who Manage

How many of the employees whom you manage are responsible for managing others? Where are the managers you manage going to fit in your new approach? If you expect them to become as hands-on as you, you have to spend some time up front talking with each of them to prepare them. You are about to radically upgrade each manager's style and practices. Focus on your managers intensely until they are up to speed and playing the new highly engaged management role you need them to play.

Lend them your copy of *It's Okay to Be the Boss*. Explain to each manager that just as you are working hard to be a better boss, she needs to do the same. Just as you are learning to talk like a performance coach, to customize your approach to every person, to meet with the employees who report to you every day, to spell out expectations more clearly, to track performance, to help employees earn what they need, your managers must do the same with their people.

From now on, you'll need to manage how they manage, every step of the way. In your regular one-on-one management meetings with them, focus on exactly how each manager is doing the hard work of managing. Ask probing questions about each employee your manager is supposed to be managing: "When did you last meet with employee #1? What did you hope to accomplish? What did you talk about? What is #2 working on? What did #3 do last week? What guidance and direction did you give #4? What are #5's current goals and deadlines? What notes did you take down in your manager's notebook? May I take a look?" If you want your managers to focus on something in particular with one or more of their employees, spell that out. If you want your managers to carry a specific message to their employees, hammer away at that message. Write it down. Put it on cards for your manager to hand out to employees. Talk it through. Role-play it.

In the early stages of teaching your managers to be hands-on, you may even want to sit in on some of your managers' one-on-one meetings with their employees to monitor and track their performance. But let the manager do the managing; don't step on the manager's toes or undermine or contradict the manager. You should simply listen and take notes, so that you can give your manager feedback after the meeting. That doesn't mean you can't give feedback directly to your manager's employee while you are there. Just make sure to keep your comments brief and turn things right back over to the manager you are managing. Sitting in on the one-on-ones will give you an up-close reality check.

Of course, you'll also need to talk to your managers about their nonmanagement tasks, projects, and responsibilities. But remember, every manager's first responsibility is managing. So that should be a huge area of focus as you manage managers.

How to Manage Your Boss

Once you're in the habit of managing yourself and your employees, you'll need to assess whether you need to also manage your boss. Sometimes you'll need to help her be as strong as you need her to be.

First, make sure you are bringing your very best to work. Arrive a little early. Stay a little late. And while you are at work, be all about the work. *Your* work, that is. Focus on playing the role assigned to you before you ever try to reach beyond that role. Focus on your tasks, your management responsibilities, your projects. Focus on doing them very well, very fast, all day long. If you really want to carry weight with your boss, this should be your primary focus every step of the way.

Second, make time every day or every week to be managed. Whether your boss realizes it or not, you need to build a regular management dialogue in the same way that you are building a management dialogue with your employees. So take the initiative to schedule regular one-on-one meetings with your boss. When trying to get more hands-on treatment from a hands-off boss, follow these rules: Meet with your boss only when you need to. When you meet, be prepared. Have a clear agenda with a small number of points you want to cover. And do your homework. If you want guidance, go in with a preliminary plan. If you have questions, try to have a few suggested answers for each question.

Third, over time, teach your boss how to manage you. Teach your boss to focus on your performance; insist that she spell out expectations, and beg for deadlines on every assignment. Help her tune in to your needs and customize her approach to you. Also make sure to customize *your* approach to your boss. And, of course, take detailed notes in every one of your one-on-one meetings and offer to share your notes with your boss.

Fourth, when you need something from your boss, ask in the form of a proposal. Don't make requests lightly, and they won't be taken lightly. Always include the following information: What is the benefit of what you are proposing? What's in it for your boss? What's in it for the team? What's in it for the organization? What's in it for the customer? If you are asking for something for yourself, you should always frame it as a quid pro quo: "I am willing to do A, B, and C to earn X, Y, or Z." Remember, if you are asking for something above and beyond, you need to offer to go above and beyond in exchange.

Fifth, always be the kind of self-starting high performer you want in your superstar employees.

It's Okay to Be the Boss.
Be a Great One!

You are the boss. You are the most important person in that workplace. What kind of boss are you going to be?

Fight the undermanagement epidemic! Create real accountability. Be the boss who says, "Great news, I'm the boss! I consider that a sacred responsibility. I'm going to make sure everything goes well around here. I'm going to help you get a bunch of work done very well, very fast, all day long. I'm going to set you up for success every step of the way. When you need something, I'm going to help you find it. When you want something, I'm going to help you earn it."

Accept your authority, take charge, and become a strong manager. You owe it to your employer. You owe it to your employees. You owe it to yourself.

It's okay to be the boss. Be a great one!

Acknowledgments

As always, I must thank first and foremost the thousands upon thousands of incredible people who have shared with me and my company over the years the lessons of your own experiences in the workplace since we first began our research in 1993. I also want to thank the very many business leaders who have expressed so much confidence in our work by hiring us and giving me such a rare opportunity to learn from the real management challenges dealt with by real managers every day in the real world. To the hundreds of thousands who have attended my keynote addresses and seminars over the years: thanks for listening, for laughing, for sharing the wisdom of your experience, for pushing me with the really tough questions, for all of your kindness, and for teaching me. My greatest intellectual debt is to the managers who have participated in our boot camps—I've learned the most about managing from helping them wrestle with their very real management problems in the real world. Special thanks to those managers whose real stories appear in this book; I've mixed up the ancillary details to help keep the stories anonymous.

To my partners in RainmakerThinking—Jeff Coombs and Carolyn Martin—thank you for your hard work and commitment and your valuable contributions to this enterprise every single day. I love you both and consider you both close and true friends. I am deeply grateful for the life-altering experience of working with each one of you. Carolyn is a gifted writer and speaker and trainer, and she has taught thousands of managers to be stronger and more effective. I've learned so much from her. Carolyn is also a light in every life she touches. Jeff has been one of my very best friends since I was sixteen, and he remains so. He is also my standing metaphor for the most valuable talent you can possibly imagine. He has run my business since 1995, and as such he is one of the first managers I taught to be strong and hands-on. I learned so much from watching Jeff become a master at being a great boss. I've also learned so much from watching Jeff be a human being. Thank you, brother Jeff.

This book is much stronger because of several other people, too. I want to thank Leah Spiro for her early advice and support. I want to thank Marion Maneker for his guidance and direction as well as his early and enthusiastic embrace of me and the book. Meanwhile, Joe Tessitore, who is the president of Collins, is my new hero because he read about my work in *Newsday* and approached me, offering me the chance to do my first major trade book since 2001. Mr. Tessitore, I want to thank you from the bottom of my heart for the honor of working with you and Collins on this book. I hope I've lived up to the confidence you placed in me.

My brilliant editor, Genoveva Llosa, took one very thorough look at my first draft and then sent me a detailed letter with step-by-step instructions for radically rewriting the whole book. She was so rigorous and thorough in her guidance and direction. She managed me like a great boss should manage an employee. She spelled out expectations clearly and vividly. She gave me a detailed checklist of to-do items. She gave me a clear deadline. Then she had me send in the chapters, one by one, as

I rewrote them. Thus, she was able to track my performance every step of the way. Now let me say, no author is happy to radically rewrite a book that he obviously thought was just fine the way he wrote it in the first place. But about halfway through the process of carrying out Genoveva's instructions, I had an epiphany. All at once I realized that she was 100 percent right. Her vision of the book was a fantastic improvement. Doing the rewrites was hard work, and Genoveva kept nipping and tucking until we finally have this infinitely better result. I have to say that editors as good as Genoveva Llosa are very uncommon. They say editors don't edit anymore. Well, Genoveva certainly does! And *wow*, she is good at it. I am immensely grateful to you for making my book so much better. Thank you.

And then there is Susan Rabiner, my agent (and my wife Debby's agent, too). I had written books before I met Susan, but I honestly feel that Susan made me an author. Susan has changed our life and our careers. She has had confidence in us all along and has always given us the bad news along with the good. Susan has taught us everything we know about writing and publishing books. Genius Susan and her genius husband, Al Fortunato, wrote *the* book on publishing nonfiction, *Thinking Like Your Editor*. Susan has a sort of Midas touch. I've never discussed an idea with Susan that didn't go through a strange alchemy. Susan transforms ideas into gold. That is her gift. We'll spend a lifelong friendship thanking Susan for helping us get our books published so wonderfully.

To my family and friends, I owe my deep and abiding thanks for allowing me to be me and for being who you are. Thanks to my parents, Henry and Norma Tulgan; my parents in-law, Julie and Paul Applegate; my nieces and nephews (from oldest to youngest): Elisa, Joseph, Perry, Erin, Frances, and Eli; my sister, Ronna, and my brother, Jim; my sister in-law, Tanya, and my brothers in-law, Shan and Tom. I love every one of you so very much.

Special thanks to my ever-loving parents for all that hard work of raising me and for being among my very closest friends to this day. I treasure the time we spend together.

Also special thanks to Frances for demonstrating for me what real micromanagement really looks like, but mostly for filling up my heart with joy and making my life complete. Thanks, Franny, for letting me help take care of you so much (an experience that has also been an unexpected source of management wisdom).

Finally, I reserve my most profound thanks always for my wife, Dr. Debby Applegate, the renowned author of *The Most Famous Man in America: The Biography of Henry Ward Beecher*. Her book is so good, such a fine specimen of writing, that it has served as a beacon of inspiration to me as I've been writing. So thanks for that, Debby. The truth is that there is nothing, absolutely nothing, I do without Debby. She is my constant adviser, my toughest critic, and my closest collaborator. This book is dedicated to Debby Applegate, the love of my life, my best friend, my smartest friend, my partner in all things, half of my soul, owner of my heart, and the person without whom I would cease to be. Thank you, my love.

Index

About the Author

Bruce Tulgan is an adviser to business leaders all over the world and a sought-after speaker and seminar leader. He is the founder of RainmakerThinking, Inc., a management training firm. Bruce is the author of the classic *Managing Generation X* as well as *Winning the Talent Wars* and eleven *Manager's Pocket Guides*. His work has been the subject of thousands of news stories around the world. He has written pieces for numerous publications, including the *New York Times*, *USA Today*, the *Harvard Business Review*, and *Human Resources*. Bruce also holds a fourth-degree black belt in classical Okinawan Ue-chi Ryu karate. He lives with his wife, Dr. Debby Applegate, author of *The Most Famous Man in America*, in New Haven, Connecticut, and Portland, Oregon. Bruce can be reached by e-mail at brucet@rainmakerthinking.com.